World Debt:
Who Is To Pay?

". . . the problem of the present debt of Latin American countries cannot be solved by only starting from mathematical calculations made by Bankers, but also taking into account the situation of those peoples that are economically exploited and impoverished. . ."
Council of the Latin American Episcopal Conference (CELAM)[1]

". . . there is a great deal of historical evidence to suggest that a society which loses its identity with posterity and which loses its positive images of the future loses also its capacity to deal with present problems, and soon falls apart."
Kenneth E. Boulding[2]

1 Final declaration of the meeting held in Bogotá, Colombia, July 1984. This and other quotations from Spanish texts, have been freely translated by the author, the present version thus being his responsibility.

2 From Fred Polak, quoted in *Towards a Steady-State Economy*, H.E. Daley (ed.), W.H. Freeman, San Francisco, 1973.

World Debt: Who Is To Pay?

Jacobo Schatan
in collaboration with
Gilda Schatan

with a Preface by
Richard Gott

Zed Books Ltd.
London and New Jersey

World Debt: Who Is To Pay? was first published in Spanish
under the title *América Latina, Deuda Externa y Desarrollo:
Un Enfoque Heterodoxo*, by Editorial El Día, Mexico, in 1985.
This is the first edition in English, published by Zed Books Ltd.,
57 Caledonian Road, London N1 9BU, UK, and 171 First
Avenue, Atlantic Highlands, New Jersey 07716, USA, in 1987.

Cover designed by Andrew Corbett.
Printed and bound in the United Kingdom
at The Bath Press, Avon.

British Library Cataloguing in Publication Data

Schatan, Jacobo
 World debt : who is to pay?
 1. Debts, External—Developing countries
 I. Title II. Schatan, Gilda III. América
 Latina, deuda externa y desarrollo. *English*
 336.3′435′091724   HJ8899

 ISBN 0-86232-688-5
 ISBN 0-86232-689-3 Pbk

Contents

Acknowledgements	vii
Note for the English Edition	viii
Preface *Richard Gott*	ix
Introduction	1
1. The Debt and its Origins	5
Early beginnings	5
The indebtedness process during the 1970s and 1980s	7
The Material Balance	16
2. The Philosophy of Foreign Indebtedness and its Main International Agents	26
The philosophy of indebtedness	26
The multilateral financial institutions	32
The responsibility of the US	39
3. The Responsibility of the Debtors	44
The flight of capital	45
Waste: A result of social irrationality	51
4. Waste and the Environment	84
Pollution and toxic effects	84
Destruction of resources	87
5. In Search of a New Path	94
The limits to consumption	95
Propaganda and the myth of progress	100
Payment of the debt	104
Beyond dependency: elimination of the structural causes of indebtedness	113
References	121
Index	125

Tables

1.1 External debt and Gross National Product of developing
      countries   8
1.2 Total debt and annual service payments of developing
      countries   9
1.3 Latin America: Total outstanding and disbursed debt at
      end of year   11
1.4 Latin America: Total outstanding and disbursed debt at
      end of year in selected countries   12
1.5 Latin America: Relationship between external debt and
      exports of goods and services   12
1.6 Latin America: Relationship between external debt and
      Gross Domestic Product   13
1.7 Latin America: Main components of the balance of
      payments   14
1.8 Latin America: Export volume and value of 18 basic
      commodities in 1982   17
1.9 Wholesale prices of 18 basic commodities in
      international markets   18
1.10 Latin America: Value and composition of one ton of the
      package of 18 basic commodities   20
1.11 Latin America: Amount of the physical remittance of
      the package of 18 basic commodities according to
      various hypotheses on export levels, repayment
      periods and interest rates   23
3.1 Mexico: Imports of goods   75
3.2 Brazil: Imports of goods   76
3.3 Chile: Imports of goods   77
3.4 Chile: Registered imports, 1980-1981   78
3.5 Chile: Imports of luxury, dispensable and replaceable
      goods   79
3.6 India: Imports of selected goods   80
3.7 Superfluous imports in three developing countries,
      1978-1981   81
3.8 Comparison of some economic indicators, India and
      three Latin American countries, 1981   82
3.9 Developing countries: Distribution of military
      expenditure by major regions, and its share in GNP,
      1970 and 1980   83

Acknowledgements

Although concern about the debt problem has been with me for a long time, it was not until the 8th Congress of the Mexican Planning Society, held in January 1984, that I could share such concern with a wider audience. Among the various round tables of the Congress, one was organized on the subject 'Austerity or Waste – Sovereignty or Dependency', which gave me the opportunity to elaborate and discuss some of the ideas that are dealt with in this book. As a corollary, my interest in deepening and widening the research on this topic was substantially increased. The result of the exercise that ensued is contained in the following pages.

I wish to thank the Mexican Planning Society for having encouraged me to take the first concrete steps; I also wish to acknowledge with thanks the generous help offered by the Department of Agricultural Economics and Resources of the University of California at Berkeley, in the form of unrestricted access to its magnificent libraries. My gratitude to Pablo Nudelman, Pedro Vuskovic and Roberto Schatan for having reviewed the manuscript and for their most valuable suggestions. I wish to underline in a very special way the close and permanent collaboration of my wife, Gilda Schatan – a journalist – whose contribution in ideas, writing, drafting and structuring the whole work was crucial for the preparation of this book.

Jacobo Schatan
Mexico, November 1984

Note for the English edition

As this translation is being made twenty-four months after the book was first written, I have taken the opportunity to update, whenever possible, the information contained in the Spanish version of the book. The most important change, however, is that corresponding to the section of Chapter 5, 'Payment of the Debt', where I introduce some materials and notions that I have prepared in the course of 1985 and 1986. Most important of these are some proposals that I presented at the International Encounter on the Foreign Debt, held in Havana, Cuba, 30 July–4 August 1985. The Epilogue, written in June 1985 for the Spanish version, has been eliminated, since its contents are mostly in the revised Chapter 5.

J.S.
1986

Preface

The history of Latin America during the 1980s has been characterized by two extraordinary developments: on the one hand what can only be described as a religious war, conducted by the United States by a variety of methods in the countries of Central America; and on the other the permanent threat of default by most of the important countries of Latin America on the debt enthusiastically incurred during the 1970s – a threat that hangs over not only the governments of the countries concerned, but over a significant number of major United States banks, and indeed over the entire Western economic system itself.

As so often happens, this latter and far more important development is shrugged off by the United States Administration as a difficulty that time, technique and good sense will overcome, while the rather less awesome threat posed to American interests by the revolution in Nicaragua and the consequent upheaval in Central America is regarded as an excuse for embarking on an ideological crusade – of an intensity and fervour that has not been seen since the days of the Vietnam War, now more than a decade ago.

In this stimulating and important book, Jacobo Schatan looks at the issue most Western governments would like to forget. Not only has he produced a useful guide to the continuing global crisis of international debt, but he has also sought to place this crisis within the continuing debate about Third World development. For long before the international banks found themselves hugely overdrawn as a result of their Third World loans, the development strategy which had called these loans into being had come under critical attack, notably in Latin America.

What makes Jacobo Schatan's book so fresh and relevant, particularly to First World eyes and to those in continents outside Latin America, is that he has taken up a number of ecological and "green" ideas and placed them at the centre of the discussion about development. So this is not just another book about the debt crisis. It asks not just why the financial loans to Latin America were stopped and whether they could be started again, but why they came in the first place, and to what use they were put. He concludes that far from trying to reconnect itself to the Western financial system, Latin America should seek to establish its own definition of development, constructing its societies with the means it has to hand.

As a long-serving official with the United Nations, and as a minister in the government of Salvador Allende, Jacobo Schatan belongs to that distinguished generation of Latin American economists which sounded an urgent note of warning throughout the 1960s and 1970s, pointing out that the external models of development being imposed on Latin America were taking the continent on a road to disaster. In the 1980s the disaster struck. First in Mexico, then in Peru, now in Brazil, the external financing structure came to an abrupt halt. Nor was this a phenomenon confined to Latin America. Throughout the Third World the process has been similar. A model of development common to Africa and Asia, as well as Latin America, has ground unceremoniously to a halt.

The significance of Jacobo Schatan's contribution to the debt debate is that he goes beyond the wringing of hands typical of liberal commentators, and questions the rationale behind the financial flows whose cut-off has occasioned the present crisis. What was the money being spent on? He foresees the need for a solution which would allow the countries of the Third World to develop their own models of development, regardless of the blandishments of the rich and powerful. Only such a project would benefit the populations of Third World countries, and the ecosystems upon which they depend.

All too often, in books about Third World development, individual nations are portrayed as victims, countries manipulated at will by the rapacity or evil motives of larger and more imperialistic states. Yet it is useful to emphasize that the debt problem has in some ways caused the situation to become reversed. The two halves of the Western hemisphere are now so economically enmeshed that, for the first time, Latin America can actually do harm to a significant segment of the United States' population.

Thirty years ago, if Jacobo Arbenz of Guatemala had chosen to expropriate the United Fruit Company (which he didn't) and with like-minded Presidents had formed a banana cartel (which actually began to happen in the 1970s), the worst that could have happened to the United States would have been a temporary shortage and disruption in the supply of bananas, and perhaps the suicide and ruin of a few corporation executives (which did happen in the 1970s). Sad, but not disastrous, and not politically upsetting. But today, if Mexico is forced to stop buying so many United States imports – not because it wants to, but because it can't afford them – a quarter of a million American jobs are at risk. It has been estimated, for example, that between 1981 and 1983, as a result of the debt crisis, the United States suffered a $33,000 million drop in exports. Almost half of this was accounted for by the decline in exports to Latin America. According to one survey, it may have cost the American economy some 400,000 jobs. So the debt crisis is, as Jacobo Schatan emphasizes, not just a crisis of Third World development, but a crisis of global proportions affecting the First World as well.

For much of the 1980s, the US obsession with Central America diverted attention from the much larger crisis looming in the hemisphere as a whole. The reason why the debt crisis has not had the treatment it deserves is that its pessimistic message is all too often subsumed under the more optimistic heading of "Latin America moves towards democracy". And it is true that a noteworthy – and noted – development of the 1980s has been the general retreat from military rule and the establishment of civilian regimes.

In South America itself, Peru, Ecuador and Bolivia had re-established civilian governments before Argentina was virtually obliged to do so in the wake of the Falklands/Malvinas debacle. Uruguay, Brazil, and even Chile, have embarked on the same road. But what is not so often remarked upon is the cause of this Gadarene rush back to barracks – a development that occurs, as has been caustically observed, "more often because of the economic and other failures of the military than for the perceived virtues of representative government."

In other words, it is the scale of the economic crisis that has forced the military to abandon ship and hand over the tiller to the civilians. Ironically, it was the earlier economic crisis – of growth rather than scarcity – that led the military to intervene in the first place in the 1960s and 1970s. For the upheavals that led to the original military seizure of power in Brazil, Argentina, Chile and Uruguay were largely due to the pressure of hitherto ignored sections of the community demanding a bigger share of the available wealth. Only the military could guarantee that the privileges of the old elite and the burgeoning middle class could be adequately safeguarded. (Peru was the exception: there the military intervened on behalf of the majority – a rare event.)

But the old growth models for development in Latin America that were current in the 1960s and 1970s have been completely overwhelmed by the debt crisis of the 1980s. It is now agreed that there is no "development" in prospect – only "crisis". Wherever you look, the authorities all agree: "The 1980s as a whole," writes William Cline, formerly deputy director for development and trade research at the US Treasury, "seem likely to be a lost decade in terms of economic growth for the major debtor countries that have been in debt-servicing difficulties."[1] Others from a similar stable write that, "the debt crisis in Latin America is clearly going to last a long time."[2] Already the evidence mounts of a dire situation getting worse. But it is also a situation that makes a fresh approach – along the lines advocated by Jacobo Schatan – both more necessary and more possible.

In 1983 there was a decline in real per capita income in Latin America of 5.6 per cent – a fall for the third year in succession. And the real GDP fell that year by 3.3 per cent, giving a cumulative decline in per capita income of 9 per cent from 1980 to 1983.

Faced with this dramatic reversal of fortune, it is hardly surprising that the Latin American military should have wished to escape from the burdens of power. For the concerns of the next decade will not be sharing out the spoils of growth, but policing the disorder caused by disappointed expectations. As William Cline dryly observes, "the sharp deceleration of growth for these major debtor countries does suggest pressure on their domestic political systems."

All this provides further evidence of the need for change of the kind that Jacobo Schatan is advocating. But a further intriguing aspect of these new developments is the fact that, for the first time, the United States itself is vulnerable to events in the Third World. American vulnerability, it is now being realized, has nothing to do with the Soviet "threat", with guerrilla movements, or with revolution and insurrection. It has everything to do with a fundamental and central flaw in the Western economic system itself.

A dozen of the largest United States banks now have loans to Latin American countries that far outstrip their capital. And some key banks are over-exposed by any standard. According to William Cline, "exposure in Brazil is approximately three quarters of the capital of Citicorp and Manufacturers Hanover, Chemical Bank, and First Interstate." Exposure in five Latin American countries – Argentina, Brazil, Mexico, Venezuela, and Chile – "exceeds 150 per cent of capital for Citicorp, Bank America, Chase Manhattan, Manufacturers Hanover, Chemical, and Crocker National." (Two British banks have an even higher degree of exposure. Lloyds Bank had 228 per cent of shareholders' funds exposed in Latin America, excluding Mexico, at the end of 1983, and the Midland Bank had 213 per cent.)

"Consider what would happen," writes William Cline, "if Argentina, Mexico and Brazil were to miss one year's payment on principal and interest..." The complete loss of one year's payments from these three countries, he says, "would cause losses equal to 28 per cent of the capital of the 9 largest United States banks." Potentially, these banks would have "to cut their losses outstanding by approximately $160,000 million as a result of a loss of $8,000 million of their capital."

And what would be the more general result? "The interest rate," notes Cline, "could be expected to rise, causing recessionary pressure... The potential would exist for economic shock waves through reduced credit availability to American businesses and consumers and, as a result, increased unemployment."

If country defaults over a wider front were to occur, writes Cline, "many major banks could become insolvent. For the 9 largest banks this would occur if just Brazil, Mexico and Argentina repudiated their debt." A truly massive failure of external debt could bring down many major banks. "Regardless of the emergency public measures that might be mounted in response, the potential economic consequences could be devastating."

This is a potential scenario, but is it actually going to happen? There are many people who think that it is. Clearly the international banking system faces great danger. In the United States, 45 banks failed in 1983 – a postwar record – and a further 25 failed in the period up to mid-May 1984. One major US bank, Continental Illinois, has already had to be rescued. A

Commonwealth expert group, chaired by Harold (Lord) Lever, has pointed out that, in the case of Continental Illinois, "the combination of Federal intervention as 'lender of the last resort' and mutual self-help between the banks avoided a collapse. But doubts remain over the ability of the system to weather a more powerful storm."[3]

Present policies, Harold Lever's group went on, "provide only a most precarious protection. The world's financial safety is balanced on a knife edge." We are not dealing, the group emphasized, "with the isolated difficulties of one or two debtor countries or of one or two creditor banks. Rather we are faced with a dangerously unstable system."

And at the moment the dangers to the system come principally from Latin America, from the countries in the United States' own backyard. "The erosion in the living standards of developing countries has pushed their peoples to the margin of tolerance," comments Harold Lever's group. And there is no prospect of amelioration. What there is a chance for in these circumstances, Jacobo Schatan would argue, is for these countries to set about doing something entirely different.

Even on the most optimistic forecast – with world recovery, IMF-approved stabilization plans, and continued lending – it would take at least a decade to restore growth and improve debt-service capacity. A forecast on these optimistic assumptions prepared in Washington "puts real GDP in the 7 major Latin American countries only 6 per cent higher in 1987 than in 1982, a 7 per cent drop in per capita income."

Much of this evidence of disaster ahead is ignored in Washington. Hopeful noises from bankers are the only ones listened to by the Reagan Administration. But in the proliferating think-tanks of the capital, a different picture is beginning to emerge. "Latin Americans are less sanguine," says a publication from the Brookings Institution, prepared by Richard Mattione and Thomas Enders.[4] Governments in Latin America, they write, "see a growth crisis. For a generation, in one of the great upward thrusts in history, Latin America grew by almost 6 per cent a year in real terms; by 1981 the economy was three times the size it had been in 1960."

But the result of all this has been an urban explosion, with the great cities of Latin America changing out of all recognition. "To take advantage of the jobs that expansion created," the Brookings report explains, "armies of people moved from the countryside to the city." Unemployment, and under-employment, had always been a problem, with a labour force still growing at the high fertility rates of the 1960s, but when economic growth came to a stop it became disastrous. "Hunger", the report emphasizes, "threatens to reach large segments of the population. Given the protests in Sao Paulo, Rio de Janeiro, Santiago and Lima, Latin American leaders wonder whether the political system will hold."

Anyone familiar with contemporary Latin America must share these doubts. "It is clear," the Brookings report continues, "that the political dangers must be taken seriously.... Only a few regiments of that great army that moved from the countryside to camp around Latin American cities will be able to return. For these people the change from 6 per cent average annual growth to stagnation or negative growth, with all that means in loss of construction and industrial jobs, has dramatic implications." Many are now pushed into destitution. "In some places hunger has become a factor, in others rioting has begun. No one can know how the situation can develop."

The report emphasizes further that "the political stresses that are appearing will put at risk the broad but shallow trend towards democracy that has marked the hemisphere in the last five years." The risk, it suggests, "is that weakened civilian or military governments will take repressive measures, not necessarily always successfully." It foresees "disorder rather than dictatorship", and "unrest throughout the hemisphere". If the crisis is of long duration, "the chances that frustration and resentment will become ungovernable are not negligible."

Calmly and judiciously, the report points out that "default must therefore be considered a real possibility at some point in the crisis for some countries, despite the absence of economic benefits from such a choice." Yet, as Jacobo Schatan argues, the social benefits to be derived from an alternative model of development, in the wake of a debt crisis, are only now beginning to be discussed.

Yet the economic impact of default on the United States would be considerable. "A moratorium on Brazil's debt", says the Brookings report, "would cost the United States $25,000 million plus 400,000 jobs ... while a moratorium throughout Latin America would raise these figures to $70,000 million and 1.1 million jobs." In 1987 Brazil did effectively declare a moratorium. The crisis is already upon us.

The solution that the Americans are calling for is for the Latin American countries to devalue their currencies and go for an export-led recovery. This would be wonderful for the United States, since the Latin Americans could then use their increased export revenues to increase their imports from the US – with the dire results that Jacobo Schatan has itemized in this book.

Yet for the strategy to succeed, as the Brookings report ruefully explains, it "would require Latin American governments to do what they have always shied away from: face up to the elite and middle classes and enterprises that have all in different ways become dependent on foreign goods and foreign travel, or on foreign education, and that tend to judge a government's performance by its ability to maintain a high exchange rate."

For here lies the rub. The only "realistic" strategy for reform and survival is bound to fail. For it would put much of the burden of the crisis on to the shoulders of the elite and the once-burgeoning middle class – the two groups that have benefited most from the imperial-controlled "development" of the last 25 years, the very people who have always rejected reforms that would adversely affect their own way of life. There is no chance that they will do so now. It is within this context that the formulations of Jacobo Schatan fall so persuasively and opportunely.

For the apocalyptic scenario for the end of the 1980s is that there will be major unrest in the principal countries of Latin America – it has already started in Peru – followed by the arrival of weak but nationalistic governments that will have little choice except to default on their debts, which will lead in turn to the weakening of the American banking system. Whatever means the United States government deploys to manage the crisis, the final result in the First World will be increased unemployment, inflation, and deepening depression – and an end to the current world trading system.

In the Third World, from amid these ruins, countries will be obliged to erect their own scenarios for future development – unaided, unassisted, and alone. Jacobo Schatan's farsighted book shows what a disastrous path Latin America has been forced to tread during the "development" years. Here he looks forward to an era in which the South is "disengaged" and "dissociated" from the North, and no longer participating in the suicidal and socially wasteful policies it had acquired from outside. His is a radical voice from the South, both "red" and "green", that deserves to be heard.

Richard Gott
March 1987

Notes

1. William Cline, *International Debt and the Stability of the World Economy,* Institute for International Economics, Washington, September 1983. And see also, William Cline, *International Debt: Systemic Risk and Policy Response,* Institute for International Economics, July 1984.

2. Thomas Enders and Richard Mattione, *Latin America: the Crisis of Debt and Growth,* Brookings Institution, Washington, March 1984.

3. Harold Lever, *The Debt Crisis and the World Economy,* report by a Commonwealth group of experts. London, July 1984.

4. Enders and Mattione, Washington, 1984.

Introduction

The early years of the 1980s witnessed the explosion of the Third World external debt crisis, which has its epicentre in the Latin American region. Whereas in the past it used to be a matter of concern for specialists in trade and financial matters, this phenomenon has acquired a universal dimension, occupying front page coverage in the most well-known newspapers with unusual frequency. Such preoccupations are shared today by political leaders, businessmen, financiers, members of national and international organizations, economists and other social scientists, and by other working people. The average Latin American is becoming conscious of the fact that she or he is bearing the weight of an external debt of over one thousand dollars each, an amount that for many working people represents several years' income.

The external debt is only one of the more visible manifestations of the profound crisis which has been affecting the Latin American region for a number of years; in its present stage the crisis represents the end of a long phase in Latin American economic development. It is a crisis that requires a fundamental redefinition of the region's external economic relations, of its internal development patterns and, in general, of prevailing social relations and values.

The crisis of the Latin American external sector is not an isolated phenomenon, associated with conjunctural problems of the world economy. On the contrary, it expresses the end of a whole system of international relations. But the Latin American crisis has its own roots; although exacerbated by external factors, it does not stem exclusively or mainly from these external factors. It could even be argued that some internal factors are responsible for the fact that repercussions deriving from external phenomena have reached the present magnitude and seriousness.

Concerning such internal roots, the economic crisis can be conceived as the crisis of the development pattern followed by Latin American societies, as well as the crisis of their basic values. The development pattern was characterized essentially by a strategy of rapid economic growth associated for a long time, in several of the Latin American countries, with a scheme of export-led industrialization. The specific forms of the industrial develop-

1

ment patterns, the inability of the agricultural sector to meet the basic food needs of the growing population, the progressive insufficiency of the productive sectors to generate gainful employment in accordance with the expansion of the labour force, the growing encroachment of foreign interests in these productive systems, the adoption of consumption and production patterns imposed by such foreign interests, the persistent tendencies towards fiscal and trade deficits, the stubbornly increasing inflationary pressures, the ever-growing income inequalities, they all demonstrate the exhaustion of the basic development pattern followed by the region.

One should add to the above list the negative effects of such a development pattern upon the ecosystem, and, more generally, upon the quality of life of the great majority of the Latin American population. The gap between social groups has been increasing, and the tragic contrast between the wasteful overconsumption of the few and the appalling underconsumption of the majority has become patent. At the same time, the 'modernization' of production and consumption schemes has contributed to the pollution of the most essential resources: air, water, soils, foodstuffs; to the deterioration of agricultural lands through erosion, desertification and salinization; to the destruction of forests and the exhaustion of aquifers; to the acceleration of the process of urbanization which, in turn, has reinforced all the previous destructive processes.

There is no doubt, however, that in the building up of those internal roots of the crisis there has been a strong dose of external influence. Together with the invasion of foreign capital (beginning with the basic infrastructure – mainly transportation, communications and mining, then in export agriculture and, more recently, in the most dynamic manufacturing branches and in information), cultural foreign penetration, particularly that coming from the US, has become a major phenomenon during the present century, reaching dramatic proportions since World War II. Consumption habits have quickly changed, especially in urban areas which, concurrently, have expanded to the point where they comprise the largest fraction of total population. Such a process, which continues unabated, has influenced decisively the pattern of industrial development in the region, having been geared to serve the 'needs' of the higher-income urban groups. Such 'needs', permeating to other population segments in obedience to the 'laws' of market expansion, have undergone a continuous process of diversification and sophistication, mainly under the impulse of foreign companies. The degree of control exerted by those corporations upon the production of goods and services, and upon the whole range of publicity mechanisms, is such that they have been able, through very refined and subtle methods, to mould the behaviour of Latin American societies, pushing them towards irresponsible superfluous consumption and hence towards waste – the sustaining pillars of western economies.

Prevailing patterns of production, industrialization, consumption, etc., in sum, of development, led many Latin American countries to increase considerably their imports of all kinds of goods since the mid-1970s, when the Western economic powers were suffering a severe recession and the world was floating in the petrodollar sea that resulted from the Yom Kippur War of October 1973. Such imports were only partially financed with export earnings; the rest came from foreign loans, for the public and the private segments of these countries. The idea was to make the big leap forward in order to emerge from the situation of 'underdevelopment' and – with the usual unfulfilled hope – to be able to repay such loans with the product of exports that would result from new investments. It was the beginning of an era of Latin American 'miracles': the Brazilian miracle, the Chilean miracle and several others. But such miracles were short-lived. External indebtedness, which was one of the pillars sustaining those economic prodigies, grew beyond all expectations. Easy money, which stimulated waste, corruption and capital flight, together with its increased cost in international financial markets, combined to push the Latin American debt to the monstrous level of approximately $400 billion recorded in 1985–6.

One could very well ask: what did the millions of 'nordestinos' (northeasterners) gain with the Brazilian 'miracle', that pushed their country to the honorific category of NIC (Newly Industrialized Country)? What did the Chilean peasants and urban workers gain from the expenditure of billions of dollars on the import of whisky, cars, electronic toys or armaments? What they – and many millions of other unfortunate Latin Americans got was a heavy mortgage that will tie them for generations, as Latin American countries will have to continue for an indefinite period remitting enormous quantities of physical and labour resources, just to pay the interest on a debt that grows day after day. Thus, the Latin American countries have become serfs of international capitalism. As in feudal times, they are chained to the obligation to export their resources to pay a debt which – unless dramatic changes take place – will never be extinguished; a debt that has been fomented and inflated by the spurious alliance of local dominant groups with the transnational banking and business interests.

At the same time, Latin American raw materials – as well as those exported by other Third World regions – are facing a severe price depression; this means that these countries are forced to increase the volume of their resource remittances in order to service their debts. Increases in interest rates and decreases in raw materials prices constitute the pincers that are strangling the Latin American region.

But the problem has an additional dimension which is seldom considered in the current debt discussions. The growing outflow of raw materials translates into an increased destruction of valuable natural resources, most of them of a finite nature, which will eventually become exhausted. The massive transfer of resources caused by increases in interest rates and other financial charges, by capital outflow, and by the prevalence of development styles that are based on the persistent increase of exports, constitute a mixture of plunder and self-destruction carried out by means of the apparently harmless instruments of the international market.

Shortly after the crisis exploded in 1982, Latin American governments began to react, trying to find some way out of the situation facing them. Quite meekly at first, consultations and meetings were held at the highest levels, continuing up to the present. But they have mainly focused on what we might call the technical and book-keeping aspects of the problem, with very little attention being paid to the examination of its internal and external roots. Some more political angles have been timidly considered only very recently, with the very strong opposition – which could be expected – from the US which favours, of course, the purely technical approaches.

It seems essential, therefore, that a much wider debate is launched so that, going beyond the superficial characteristics of the crisis, attempts are made at reaching its central causes, as well as at finding solid and enduring solutions, not just the cosmetic ones being proposed and considered by the international leadership. It is urgent, therefore, to make systematic and thorough studies of the phenomena and processes mentioned above, and others related to them. There should, however, be a new approach, so that new propositions can be formulated. These should represent a general option that is viable both technically and politically. It will be necessary to present, frankly and clearly, these desired development options and lifestyles. It is probable, perhaps inevitable, that such options will lead to a gradual disconnection of the Third World from the countries of the 'developed' world, and, at the same time, to closer links among Third World countries themselves. We believe that, in the case of Latin America, the external debt crisis could serve as a trigger for that indispensable process of change in development patterns that will lead to a more advanced stage in human relations.

In the following pages we explore, albeit very briefly, a few of the fundamental aspects of such a problem. We attempt in very broad terms to explain *why* there is such a monstrous debt, *who* originated it and *how*, which are the forces and ideologies that sustain and aggravate the situation of indebtedness, and that are responsible for its long-term consequences, *how* such a situation is deeply embedded in the overall development patterns followed by Latin American countries, and, finally, *which* might be the ways to get out of the profound crisis affecting this region.

It is needless to stress the numerous limitations of the present exploration: there are many gaps to fill; assumptions or conclusions that are highly debatable; figures that are not sufficiently precise, etc. Indeed, we do not pretend that our arguments are complete and mathematically irrefutable. Our aim is more modest than that; we only wish to contribute some ideas, reflexions and preoccupations that may be useful for the much-needed in-depth study and discussion referred to above.

1 The Debt and its Origins

Early beginnings

It is interesting to note that the present Latin American debt situation is not an entirely new phenomenon. During the 1870s something similar happened when, at the main financial centre of that time, the London Stock Exchange, a feverish external lending race took place, caused by the great profitability of such operations. Although repayments stopped occasionally, the flow of capital from the Centre to the Periphery[1] continued without interruption. For various reasons a good number of South American countries, besides Egypt, Turkey, and Greece, decided by the end of that decade to suspend, partially or totally, payment of interest on their debts. Nevertheless, ten years later the lending operations to South America were resumed, and this region became the main consumer of European capital. Apparently, profits generated by these loans were so vast that lenders could afford to absorb such sporadic losses! It is estimated that the amount of interest and profits remitted by the colonies in Asia and Africa, and by the independent countries of Latin America between 1815 and 1914 was higher than the absolute increase of their outstanding overall debt with the metropolitan centres.[2] Equally, in many countries the rate of indebtedness and service payment greatly exceeded that of export growth. In the case of Argentina, for instance, while foreign trade grew by about five times in the 30–year period from 1881–85 to 1910–14, foreign debt services increased by around eight times. Many testimonies coincide in pointing out the similarity between 19th Century and present-day monetary policies. For example, during the last century many governments used to deposit vast amounts of money in the London and Paris markets; this capital was used by the European banks to increase their foreign loans, including loans to the depositor countries. It is needless to emphasize the huge profitability of such operations![3]

In 19th Century Latin America, the generation of the indebtedness process, and its further development, gave rise to a capitalist class without the direct responsibility for a genuine internal capital accumulation, that might have set in motion a locally-controlled process of further capital accumulation and technological management. As in other regions of the world, the Latin American élites found in free trade the reply to their modernization needs and the way to keep and consolidate their economic and political power.[4]

During and after World War I the international financial markets stopped functioning adequately. Operations in Latin America, however, were not renewed when the war ended. Financial centres, once markets went back to normality, focused on the needs of the industrial countries, whose financial requirements were constantly increasing as a result of reconstruction efforts and their subsequent economic expansion. During several decades, and until many years after World War II, those financial centres had relatively small capital surpluses to lend to Latin American nations and to the Third World in general. This did not mean, however, that financial flows between the Centre and the Periphery stopped during those years. On the contrary, they increased, though not as bank loans but rather as direct investments. After 1945, when the main multilateral financial organizations were created (e.g. IMF and World Bank), official lending operations began, adding to bilateral financing (i.e. from government to government), a practice that acquired great relevance during a good part of the postwar period.

The import-substitution-led industrialization process, which had been greatly stimulated by the depression of the 1930s, acquired additional force, becoming the engine of the economic growth process in countries of the Periphery after World War II. When the war ended, the US reinstated a number of assistance programmes, which began to support the new industrializing drive. The increase in world demand for raw materials, as a result of the Korean War, and the corresponding price increases, greatly stimulated export activities in Latin America and in other regions. With the additional resources thus obtained, these countries embarked on vast programmes of industrialization and expansion of their basic infrastructure, which required huge imports of equipment, technology, and other goods and services; these, in turn, necessitated vast amounts of external financing. Thus emerged the mechanism of financial-technological dependency which, according to Corm[5] would lead, at a later stage, to a situation in which transnational corporations and international financial markets became the kingpins of Third World development and modernization mechanisms, while financial institutions turned into the arbiters of the socio-political problems of the Third World.

The indebtedness process during the 1970s and 1980s

It was not until the 1970s that private international banking 'rediscovered' Latin America. When the first oil shock took place at the end of 1973, as a consequence of the Yom Kippur War in the Middle East, and oil prices skyrocketed, a financial process began which, for the period 1974–80, can be summarized as follows.

1. The most important oil-exporting countries, not being able to utilize domestically the vast financial surpluses generated by oil price increases, made huge deposits in various OECD financial institutions.

2. At the same time, a good number of middle- and high-income oil-importing nations – particularly those with a higher degree of industrialization – decided to accelerate their rates of economic growth, notwithstanding the increase in oil prices; that policy contrasted sharply with the 'stagflation' situation prevailing in the OECD countries.

3. In order to carry out their economic expansion policies many developing countries requested huge loans from OECD commercial banks, so as to be able to make massive imports of all kinds of goods, apart from oil; in particular chemical products, foodstuffs and capital goods (although, as we shall see later, they also imported vast amounts of superfluous goods; equally, corruption and capital flight were vigorously stimulated).

4. The OECD banks, with great liquidity and a weak domestic demand for funds, started a wild competition to export capital to the more dynamic of the less-developed nations, which, at that moment, decided to apply to the international private banking system to obtain the money required to implement their expansive economic policies.

5. In order to diminish the risks of those operations, the international private banks decided to change the terms and conditions of the loans, shifting from the fixed rates of interest that had prevailed until then, to variable rates. The borrowing nations accepted such changes under the influence of the aggressive marketing techniques employed by the banks, which included attractive offers that appeared to be to their benefit, without realizing the grave harm that they would suffer in the future. What at the beginning appeared as a mere technical innovation came to be a real trap, since any increase in the interest rate would apply to the total outstanding debt and not only to the new loans.

In a second period, starting shortly before the advent of the Reagan Administration in the US (January 1981), the above situation changed completely. Alongside a world economic recession, inflation became increasingly acute in the US and other industrial nations, and rates of interest escalated. The economic recession in the central nations motivated a sharp drop in prices of raw materials exported by Third World countries, precisely at the moment when the financial charges due to interest payments became heavier, and when the flow of fresh capital to the Third World began to slacken. Thus by 1982 the crisis in Mexico acquired full force, followed by similar crises in other Latin American countries, as well as in other regions of the world. The crisis became universal. Latin American nations abruptly had to compress their imports in order to be able to continue paying their debt services and, for the first time, Latin America became an important net capital exporter. Figures show with dramatic clarity the development of the indebtedness process since the early 1970s. According to World Bank data (see table 1.1, below) total outstanding and disbursed debt of developing countries as a whole trebled between 1970 and 1976, and more than trebled between 1976 and 1984, when it approached $700 billion. If short-term debt is included, total external obligations of developing countries amounted to the astounding figure of $900 billion in 1984. Considering that the indebtedness process has continued unabated during 1985 and 1986, although at a slower pace, the developing world's external burden probably surpassed the $1,000 billion mark by the end of 1986.

OECD data (which we have available only until 1982) confirms the debt progression indicated above: total disbursed debt of developing nations went up eight times between 1971 and 1982, from $90 billion to $626 billion. OECD figures are also quite illustrative about the sources of loans.

Table 1.1
External debt and Gross National Product of developing countries

	Total GNP	Total Debt[a]	Total Interest Payments[b]	Relationships: Debts/GNP	Interest Payment/GNP
	(in $ billion)			*(in percentages)*	
1970	482	68	2.4	14.1	0.5
1974	916	141	7.3	15.4	0.8
1976	1,127	204	9.0	18.1	0.8
1978	1,490	313	16.4	21.0	1.1
1980	2,059	430	32.9	20.9	1.6
1981	2,178	488	41.4	22.4	1.9
1982	2,076	546	47.7	26.3	2.3
1983	1,981	620	45.6	31.3	2.3
1984	2,030	686	56.8	33.8	2.8

[a]Total Outstanding and Disbursed Debt of Developing Countries. It does not include short-term debt and other external obligations of developing nations. When these are included figures for overall external obligations go up by around 40 per cent. According to World Bank data, the grand total for 1980 was $610 billion, while that estimated for 1984 was $895 billion.

[b]It is most likely that the concept of 'interest payments' included under this column corresponds to the disbursed debt figures appearing in the second column of this table and not to the overall external obligations of developing nations. It is also likely, therefore, that overall interest payments made by these countries must have been much larger than those recorded by this table.

Source: World Bank, *World Development Report 1985.*

Table 1.2
Total debt and annual service payments of developing countries
(in $ billion)

		1971	1975	1977	1979	1980	1981	1982
A.	Total disbursed debt	90	180	274	406	465	530	626
	Concessional	33	57	73	93	103	116	131
	Non-concessional	57	123	201	313	362	414	495
	Originating in capital markets	20	61	103	162	190	222	265
B.	Total service	11.0	25.8	42.1	75.6	86.9	109.3	131.3
	Interest	3.3	9.3	12.9	26.0	37.2	48.5	60.1
	Amortization	7.7	16.5	29.2	49.6	49.7	60.8	71.2
	Concessional	1.7	3.1	3.9	4.5	5.4	6.1	6.9
	Non-concessional	9.3	22.7	38.2	71.1	81.5	103.2	124.4
	of which: Capital markets	2.7	9.5	17.8	38.3	43.4	57.5	67.0

Source: OECD, *External Debt of Developing Countries, 1982 Surveys* (Paris, 1982).

As can be seen in table 1.2, the major portion of the increment corresponded to commercial loans, or 'non-concessional' as they are known in financial jargon: of the $536 billion by which the total external debt of the developing countries expanded in eleven years (1971–82), nearly $440 billion – about 80 per cent – represented commercial loans, whereas those granted by official credit institutions, which enjoy more favourable conditions (hence 'concessional') increased by somewhat less than $100 billion. Thus, private capital markets became the main foreign financial source for the Third World: by 1982 they supplied almost half of the total gross disbursed debt, while in 1971 that proportion had been only one-fifth. This trend is supported by World Bank data. These show that official development assistance went up from $8 billion in 1970 to $33.6 billion in 1983, while non-concessional flows sextupled during the same period, from $11 billion to $64 billion (annual figures in both cases).

Concessional loans granted by governments and multilateral lending organizations have a much lower cost than those of commercial banks. Thus, the process of 'commercialization' of the external debt had a decisive impact on the magnitude of the annual payments to service the debt. As can be seen in table 1.2, total service increased twelve-fold during the period

1971–82, but the fraction corresponding to interest alone rose twenty-fold. It is worth noting that almost the whole of the service (amortization of principal plus interest) was attached to 'non-concessional' loans, their 'extraction' passing from $9 billion to $124 billion in only eleven years. This was, obviously, the result of the juxtaposition of a higher proportion of commercial loans and the much faster increase in interest rates applied by commercial banks. Whereas the average rate for debts contracted at fixed rates (mostly concessional), went up from 4.4 to about 8 per cent between 1972–73 and 1982 (OECD data), the average rate for loans with floating rates (mainly 'non-concessional') augmented from 8.3 to 17.5 per cent during that period. In relative terms (i.e. the proportion by which the above rates increased) the change was not so dissimilar – 82 per cent in the first case and 110 per cent in the second. But what really counts is the differential in absolute percentage points: 3.6 points in the first case and more than 9 points in the other. This is where the trap lies! (The growing participation of the multinational private banks in loans to the Third World, and the brutal increase in interest rates, are reflected in the accelerated growth of the banks' profits derived from their foreign operations).[5]

Information provided by the World Bank in its 1985 World Development Report confirms such a nefarious trend for the Third World countries. The proportion of interest payments in total Gross National Product (GNP) of all developing nations went up from 0.5 per cent in 1970 to 2.8 per cent in 1984, as can be seen in table 1.1. Total interest payments, which probably include only that part corresponding to the disbursed debt and not to the total external obligations, increased by 24 times during that period, from $2.4 billion to nearly $57 billion. The implicit average interest rate, which was 3.5 per cent in 1970, had risen to over 8 per cent in the 1980s. Although interest rates declined after 1982, to reach a level of around 11 per cent (prime rate) at the end of 1984, 9.5 per cent at the end of 1985, and 7.5 per cent by September 1986, the possibility that they may start climbing again in the not-too-distant future cannot be ruled out.

The process explained above has affected the Latin American countries even more decisively, as they are among the major debtors in the world. Figures for 19 Latin American countries show a global debt level of around $370 billion in 1985 (see table 1.3); if Cuba and other Caribbean nations are included, the total would probably stretch beyond the $380 billion mark, that is, almost one-half of all the Third World's foreign debt. Fifteen years earlier the Latin American debt had been only $23 billion, by 1977 it had passed the $100 billion mark and by 1983 it was close to $350 billion. Only six countries are responsible for more than four-fifths of the Latin American debt (see table 1.4) with a total that is estimated to have reached by end-1985 something over $325 billion: Brazil, $105bn; Mexico, $100bn; Argentina, $50bn; Venezuela, $35bn; Chile, $22bn; Peru $14bn. Currently, these countries bear the heaviest burden in total debt servicing: according to OECD data, their aggregate disbursement on this account surpassed in 1982 the figure of $50 billion.

As can be seen in table 1.3, most of the increment in total indebtedness came from commercial loans, which went up twenty-fold between 1970 and 1985; official credit, instead, moved up slowly, with an eight-fold increase during those 15 years. Other indicators show, in an equally dramatic way, the external situation of Latin America. According to data from the UN Economic and Social Commission (CEPAL), the ratio of Debt to Exports was 3.2 to 1 in 1984, a considerable jump from the 1.9 to 1 ratio of only

Table 1.3
Latin America: Total outstanding and disbursed debt at end of year[a]

	Total Debt	*Debt with official sources*		*Debt with private sources*[b]	
	($ billion)	*($ billion)*	*(Percentage of total debt)*	*($ billion)*	*(Percentage of total debt)*
1970	23	8	36	15	64
1971	26	9	36	17	64
1972	30	10	34	20	66
1973	40	12	28	28	72
1974	56	14	25	42	75
1975	75	16	22	59	78
1976	98	18	18	80	82
1977	116	21	18	95	82
1978	151	25	16	127	84
1979	182	27	15	157	85
1980	223	31	14	198	86
1981	278	34	12	246	88
1982	318	40	12	278	88
1983	344	51	15	293	85
1984	360	57	16	303	84
1985	368	65	18	303	82

[a]Includes Argentina, Bolivia, Brazil, Colombia, Costa Rica, Chile, Ecuador, El Salvador, Guatemala, Haiti, Honduras, Mexico, Nicaragua, Panama, Paraguay, Peru, Dominican Republic, Uruguay and Venezuela. Estimates comprise long, medium and short-term debts, and debts with financial institutions that report to the Bank for International Settlements that are not officially guaranteed. Debts with other financial institutions and export loans that are not officially guaranteed are excluded.
[b]All short-term debts are presumed to be with private sources.

Source: CEPAL, on the basis of data from World Bank, Bank for International Settlements, Inter-American Development Bank.

seven years earlier. In a great number of countries the external debt grew much more rapidly than did their exports. This resulted in a trebling of the debt : export ratio for Argentina, and in the doubling of that for Chile in just six years (see table 1.5).

The external debt has also grown disproportionately in relation to the Gross Domestic Product (GDP) in a number of Latin American countries,

Table 1.4
Latin America: Total outstanding and disbursed debt at end of year in selected countries
(in $ billion)

	1978	1980	1981	1982	1983	1984
Argentina	12.5	27.2	35.7	43.6	46.5	49.0
Brazil	52.3	68.4	78.6	87.6	96.5	102.4
Chile	6.7	11.1	15.5	17.2*	17.4*	18.4*
Mexico	33.9	50.7	74.9	88.3	92.1	95.9
Peru	9.3	9.6	9.7	11.1	12.4	13.3
Venezuela	16.4	26.5	28.4	30.5	33.5	31.3
Other countries	19.8	29.0	34.9	40.1	45.6	49.4
Total	150.9	222.5	277.7	318.4	344.0	359.7

Source: CEPAL, Statistical Yearbook 1985.

Table 1.5
Latin America: Relationship between external debt and exports of goods and services
(Index: Exports = 100)

	1977	1979	1981	1982	1983	1984
Latin America	191	202	213	309	338	317
Argentina	125	192	271	338	365	. . .
Brazil	252	297	255	341	345	. . .
Chile	188	158	226	289	317	. . .
Mexico	341	248	232	253	270	. . .
Peru	294	175	205	234	238	. . .
Venezuela	106	154	137	172	134	. . .

Country figures for 1984 not available.
Source: CEPAL, various publications

reaching levels that can be considered truly unbearable. Thus, as shown in table 1.6, the relationship in the case of Argentina went up from about 15 per cent in 1977 to over 40 per cent in 1983; in Chile and Venezuela such ratio increased from around 35 per cent to a staggering 60 per cent during the same period. For the region as a whole the situation appears slightly better, although by 1985 the average ratio had climbed to over 43 per cent, one-fifth higher than that recorded in 1983. This indicates that 1985 ratios for individual countries must have dramatically increased as well.

Although these last four or five years have witnessed a serious aggravation of the Latin American foreign debt situation, premonitory signs could be observed much earlier. For instance, in its 1969 Annual Economic Survey, CEPAL pointed out that external borrowing policies applied by Latin American nations had originated large increases in foreign capital services, thereby absorbing a growing proportion of export earnings of this region. The figures were quite illustrative:

> Between 1958 and 1968 income originating in the exportation of goods and services grew at a yearly rate of 4.7 per cent, while total foreign capital services (interest, profits, amortization and depreciation) increased at an annual rate of 7.9 per cent.

Such a discrepancy, lasting many years and continuing throughout the 1970s, could not but give rise to an enormous debt. Table 1.7 shows the basic components of the balance of payments for Latin America between 1950 and 1984 (selected years). It can be clearly seen from this table that, until 1980, the growing deficits in current account were more than compensated by much higher net capital inflows, although an increasing proportion of these were bank loans, whose cost, as we saw, was constantly

Table 1.6
Latin America: Relationship between external debt and Gross Domestic Product
(Index: GDP = 100)

	1977	1979	1981	1982	1983	1984*	1985*
Latin America	23.9	28.4	32.2	33.7	35.7	42.7	43.2
Argentina	14.7	26.2	38.4	39.7	41.1	. . .	. . .
Brazil	22.3	25.7	26.5	28.5	31.6	. . .	. . .
Chile	34.8	37.8	47.6	60.9	60.2	. . .	. . .
Mexico	23.4	24.0	30.2	31.5	33.0	. . .	. . .
Peru	36.9	35.0	31.0	33.6	40.8	. . .	. . .
Venezuela	36.4	63.9	66.1	65.3	61.8	. . .	. . .

Country figures for 1984 and 1985 not available.
*Estimated by the author on the basis of indirect CEPAL data.
Source: CEPAL, various publications.

Table 1.7
Latin America*: Main components of the balance of payments
($ million)

	Exports of Goods and Services	Imports of Goods and Services	Balance of Trade	Payments of profits, interest and other remittances (net)	Balance in Current Account	Balance in Capital Account	Balance of Payments
1960	10,059	10,043	16	-1,267	-1,251	1,226	-25
1970	18,200	18,802	-602	-2,811	-3,412	4,382	969
1975	44,309	52,784	-8,475	-5,659	-14,130	14,775	645
1980	113,708	123,321	-9,613	-18,528	-28,144	30,259	2,115
1981	122,145	134,757	-12,612	-27,834	-40,448	37,959	-2,490
1982	108,637	111,177	-2,540	-39,809	-42,349	20,888	-21,461
1983	107,641	81,691	25,950	-34,925	-8,977	3,369	-5,609
1984**	113,884	78,953	34,930	-35,956	-1,029	10,303	9,275

*Includes Argentina, Barbados, Bolivia, Brazil, Colombia, Costa Rica, Chile, Ecuador, El Salvador, Guatemala, Guyana, Haiti, Honduras, Jamaica, Mexico, Nicaragua, Panama, Paraguay, Peru, Dominican Republic, Suriname, Trinidad and Tobago, Uruguay, Venezuela.

**Excludes Barbados, Guyana, Jamaica, Suriname, Trinidad and Tobago.

Source: CEPAL, Statistical Yearbook for Latin America and the Caribbean, 1985. Table 228. 1984: other CEPAL publications.

rising. Thus one can explain why in a few years the net remittance of profits and interests grew from less than $3 billion (1970) to nearly $40 billion (1982). In just five years, 1980–1984, the Latin American region paid about $160 billion under the item 'net profits, interest and other remittances'. During this quinquennium the total negative balance in current account was $117 billion, due to the large surpluses in the trade balance recorded in the latter part of this period; the balance in the capital account totalled about $100 billion. If we assume that in 1986 the net capital inflow was positive once again, we may arrive at the conclusion that, on the whole, the region has come out roughly even during the period 1980–86. However, it is worth noting what has happened during the last four years of this period. In 1981 the net capital inflow, although at a record level of $38 billion, was hardly sufficient to offset an enormous negative balance in the current account, and the balance of payments closed with a small deficit of $2.5 billion, the first of such deficits in a very long time. But in 1982, when the Mexican crisis broke out, the net capital inflow fell to half its previous level, and in 1983 descended to a level that had not been recorded since the 1960s. In 1984 the inflow of capital increased somewhat, to a level still not higher than that recorded ten years earlier.

As a result of such financial movements, the balance of payments reached in 1982 the unprecedented negative level of −$21 billion; the following year this disastrous situation was controlled to some extent, thanks to the huge surplus in the balance of trade, which resulted from a drastic curtailing of imports. As can be seen in table 1.7, the total value of imports began to decline after 1981, but the most important diminution took place between 1982 and 1983, with a decrease of nearly $30 billion to a level close to $80 billion, which remained fairly stable throughout 1984 and 1985.

With exports at well over $100 billion, the positive balance of trade has permitted the region to continue paying the interest on its foreign debt. Thus, for the first time in a long time, Latin America became a net capital exporter. Also for the first time in many decades this region was covering its current account deficits with its own resources. This happened against the will, plans, and expectations of Latin American leaders. Traditionally, such deficits had been amply compensated for by external financing, this having been an important factor in the rapid debt growth, as indicated earlier. But, at the same time, the structure of the debt changed significantly, due to the modification in the sources of financing. While up to the mid-1970s loans with official origin – governmental or multilateral – constituted the largest proportion, after that date lending from commercial banks became the major source. Besides, private debt grew very rapidly: from 36 per cent of the total debt in 1973 it passed to 42 per cent in 1981. Linked to this change we can observe a marked shrinkage in the average length of debt periods, since short-term loans contracted with commercial banks increased so much. In only two years, between 1979 and 1981, the proportion of short-term loans shot up from 25 to 30 per cent of all loans.

Conversely, the proportion of official financial flows diminished considerably: from 54 per cent in 1971–73 to 34 per cent in 1979.

The Material Balance

So far, we have examined the Latin American debt problem in purely monetary terms, which is the traditional way of dealing with such issues. But the monetary sign, be it the dollar, the yen or the mark, represents a given amount of physical and human resources. When countries remit abroad a number of those dollars, marks or yen, to pay the interest and amortization of their debts, they are in fact sending away a given amount of their physical resources and the human labour incorporated in them. Since the Third World is not a significant exporter of services (except for tourism in certain countries), these nations have no other way but to export physical goods in order to obtain the currency required to service their debts. The volume of goods to be exported for each service unit will obviously depend on the international prices of those products that the debtor country may be in a position to export. Thus, for example, if copper prices are quoted at $1,500 per metric ton, a country like Chile or Peru will have to remit abroad about 660 tons of this metal for each million dollars of service payment.

The total amount of goods remitted to service the debt will naturally vary according to the fluctuations affecting each of the main components of the equation: the unit export prices, the composition of exports, the cost of money (i.e. the rate of interest and other financial costs charged by the lenders), and the global amount of the debt.

Prices of goods and those of money have evolved in a diametrically opposite fashion, to the obvious detriment of Third World countries. That is, terms of trade between money and goods exported by the North and exportable resources of the Third World have seriously deteriorated. Or, expressed in a different way: the glass beads brought by the neo-conquerors in the present form of electronic gadgets, luxurious superfluous manufactures, armaments, sophisticated technology, and other things of the kind, have been overvalued in comparison with the metals and other resources extracted from the neo-colonies, while at the same time the cost of money lent to them to buy those neo-glass beads has increased.

To obtain a more graphic understanding of the meaning of the present situation of Latin American foreign indebtedness, and the subjection that its annual service implies, we have designed a 'package' with the 18 main basic commodities exported by this region (in 1982). Listed according to the Spanish alphabetical order they are: cotton, sugar, bauxite, coffee, shrimp, beef, copper, tin, fishmeal, iron ore, wool, maize, oil, bananas, lead, soya, wheat, and zinc. We have calculated the amount of the debt and services in terms of that package, the unit of which we shall designate as MAPRAL, the acronym for Materias Primas de América Latina (Latin American Raw Materials).

Table 1.8
Latin America[a]: Export volume and value of 18 basic commodities in 1982

Product	Volume		Value	
	thousand tons	*per cent*	*$ million*	*per cent*
Cotton	325	0.12	473	0.97
Sugar	5,116	1.93	1,059	2.18
Bananas	2,141	0.81	801	1.65
Bauxite	1,067	0.40	222	0.46
Coffee	2,464	0.93	5,143	10.58
Shrimp	236	0.09	323	0.66
Beef	1,084	0.42	1,528	3.14
Copper	1,484	0.56	2,191	4.51
Tin	22	0.01	278	0.57
Fishmeal	570	0.21	202	0.43
Iron ore	77,115	29.10	2,005	4.12
Wool	201	0.08	428	0.88
Maize	6,573	2.48	585	1.20
Oil	152,801	57.56	29,949	61.62
Lead	399	0.15	216	0.44
Soya	9.073	3.42	2,223	4.57
Wheat	4,251	1.60	676	1.39
Zinc	356	0.13	306	0.63
Total 18 products	**265,278**	**100.00**	**48,608**	**100.00**

[a]23 countries (Cuba is excluded).

Source: IMF, *International Financial Statistics.*

Table 1.9
Wholesale prices of 18 basic commodities in international markets

	1976–77 (average)	1980	1981	1982	1983	1985 (July)
Cotton (¢/lb)[a]	64.80	81.30	72.02	60.03	68.43	59.90
Sugar (¢/lb)	9.79	28.67	16.89	8.41	8.47	3.25
Bananas (¢/lb)	12.02	17.01	18.20	16.99	19.46	17.25
Bauxite ($/ton)	126.05	212.45	216.34	208.35	179.54	164.28[c]
Coffee (Brazil, NY, ¢/lb)	208.31	208.79	186.44	143.68	142.75	130.81
Shrimp ($/lb)	3.69	4.60	4.41	6.21	6.00	4.59
Beef (US ports, all origins, ¢/lb)	70.22	125.19	112.12	108.39	110.67	93.05
Copper (London, ¢/lb)	61.51	99.18	78.78	67.07	72.13	66.90
Tin (London, all origins, ¢/lb)	417.23	761.71	643.98	579.65	589.14	578.50
Fish meal (Hamburg, all origins, $/ton)	414.55	504.42	467.50	353.75	452.50	254.00
Iron ore min. ($/ton)	21.80	27.24	24.62	26.21	23.78	22.70
Wool (New Zealand, greasy, ¢/kilo)	202.55	275.33	243.55	212.98	196.89[b]	184.70[d]
Maize (Chicago, ¢/bushel)	2.45	3.00	3.16	2.52	3.23	2.79
Oil (Saudi Arabia, $/barrel)	11.95	27.60	32.03	32.03	28.05	27.80[e]
Lead (London, ¢/lb)	24.10	41.19	33.00	24.62	19.27	18.30
Soya ($/ton)	255.00	296.25	288.42	244.50	281.67	223.00
Wheat (US, Gulf ports, ¢/bushel)	3.22	4.70	4.76	4.36	4.28	3.50
Zinc (London, ¢/lb)	29.45	34.46	38.60	33.69	34.73	34.20

[a] All quotations are expressed in US currency
[b] Third quarter
[c] March
[d] June
[e] May

Sources: IMF, *International Financial Statistics.*

This is a simplification we have made for purely illustrative purposes, since those 18 commodities represent only three-fifths of all Latin American exports; the other two-fifths are manufactured goods, intermediate products, other raw materials, foodstuffs, etc., many of which have a higher export unit value. Besides, exports of manufactures have been increasing more rapidly than exports as a whole, particularly in Brazil and a few other countries. However, since it would be extremely difficult and cumbersome to work with the whole range of exported products in physical terms – something that is not at all justified for the type of work we are attempting here – we believe that such simplification does not invalidate the present exercise. Moreover, the total export value of the 18 commodities selected was, in 1982 – the year chosen for our calculations – quite similar to the service of the debt (around $45 billion).

In order to determine the composition of one MAPRAL we calculated for each product a share corresponding to its respective proportion within the total volume of the 18 commodities exported in 1982 (see table 1.8); we then used the individual commodity prices in different reference periods (see table 1.9), to obtain the average value of one MAPRAL in various years. They turned out to be the following: $136 in 1976–77, $217 in 1980, $191 in 1983, $171 in 1985 (July) (see table 1.10). Although we do not possess firm data on the prices of most raw materials for 1986, we attempted to estimate the MAPRAL's value for that year in order to record the very sharp drop in oil prices that took place during the early months, remaining at approximately one-half its 1985 level throughout all of 1986. The result came to $128, a figure lower than that recorded ten years earlier.

The main factor explaining the increase in value of the MAPRAL between 1976–77 and 1983 was the rise in the price of petroleum: if this commodity is excluded from the calculation, the average price index for the 17 remaining commodities was the same in both years, to decline sharply afterwards.

The next step was the conversion of the total dollar value of the foreign debt and its annual services into MAPRALs, using the average prices mentioned above. In order to estimate the total gross outflow* of raw materials during the debt repayment period we assumed that total service would continue to be $45 billion throughout the whole repayment period. To determine the length of such period, and, therefore, the amounts to be devoted to amortization of the principal and to interest payment, we used

---

* We speak of *gross* because, in the case of non-renewable resources, we ought to discount the inflow of materials that come incorporated in manufactured goods, which eventually could be recycled and therefore utilized once again. But the calculation of the *net* outflow would be an extremely laborious exercise which is beyond the illustrative scope of the present work. One can guess, however, that the amounts of iron, copper, etc., that arrive in the form of manufactures (net imports) are only a small fraction of those which leave the region as raw materials. It would be interesting, however, to verify this hypothesis by means of empirical studies on the balance of non-renewable materials.

Table 1.10
Latin America: Value and composition of one ton of the package of 18 basic commodities

Commodity	Weight[b] (kg)	Price (¢/kg)				Value of package			
		1976–77	1980	1983	1985 (July)	1976–77	1980	1983	1985 (July)
Cotton[a]	1.22	142.6	178.9	150.5	131.8	1.74	2.18	1.84	1.60
Sugar	19.30	21.5	63.1	18.6	7.1	4.15	12.18	3.59	1.37
Bananas	8.08	26.4	37.4	42.8	37.9	2.13	3.02	3.46	3.06
Bauxite	4.02	12.6	21.2	18.0	16.4	0.51	0.85	0.72	0.66
Coffee	9.30	458.3	459.3	314.0	287.8	42.62	42.71	29.20	26.76
Shrimp	0.89	811.1	1,012.0	1,320.0	1,009.8	7.22	9.00	11.75	8.99
Beef	4.19	154.5	275.4	243.5	204.7	6.47	11.54	10.20	8.57
Copper	5.60	135.3	218.3	158.7	147.1	7.58	12.22	8.89	8.24
Tin	0.08	917.9	1,675.8	1,296.1	1,272.7	0.73	1.34	1.04	1.02
Fishmeal	2.15	41.5	50.4	45.2	25.4	0.89	1.08	0.98	0.55
Iron ore	291.00	2.2	2.7	2.4	2.3	6.40	7.86	6.98	6.69
Wool	0.76	202.5	275.3	196.9	184.7	1.54	2.09	1.50	1.40
Maize	24.80	8.6	10.6	11.3	9.7	2.13	2.63	2.80	2.40
Petroleum[c]	575.60	7.0	16.2	16.4	15.5	40.29	93.25	94.40	89.22
Lead	1.50	53.2	90.6	42.4	40.2	0.80	1.36	0.64	0.60
Soya	34.23	25.5	29.6	28.2	22.3	8.73	10.13	9.65	7.63
Wheat	16.04	11.2	16.5	15.0	12.2	1.80	2.65	2.40	1.96
Zinc	1.34	64.8	75.8	76.4	75.2	0.87	1.01	1.02	1.00

Total	**1,000.00**	136.60	217.10	191.06	171.72
Without petroleum	**424.40**	96.31	123.85	96.66	82.50
Indices:					
Total package	100	100	159	140	126
Without petroleum	100	100	129	100	86

a Listing corresponds to alphabetical order in Spanish.
b In one tonne of the package.
c If we take May 1986 prices, oil participation in the package could go down to only $46; with the other prices remaining constant, the total value of the package's ton would be $128.50.

two hypotheses on interest rates: one of 10 per cent, which is similar to the 1985 average, and a second of 6 per cent, which is similar to that prevailing in the mid-1970s. Under the first hypothesis, total interest payments would be some $40 billion in the initial year and amortization would be $5 billion; the repayment period would thus be 23 years. Under the second hypothesis, the amount devoted to interest in the first year would decline to $24 billion the amortization would climb to $21 billion, thus permitting the repayment of the debt in only 13 years.

But the exercise cannot stop here. We have also to consider the outflow of resources required to provide the currency needed to import goods and services, ruling out further indebtedness. For this reason we had to estimate the level of exports needed to cover the cost of imports plus the debt services. If imports are kept at a level similar to that of recent years, about $80 billion, much lower than those recorded in 1980, 1981 and 1982, but similar to the levels prevailing in the late 1970s, total exports would have to climb to an annual average of $125 billion, a figure only slightly higher than actual export figures in 1984 and 1985. We also assumed that the 18 basic commodities would continue to represent 60 per cent of total exports, although we reiterate the limitations of such an assumption, given the fact already indicated that manufactures' participation in total exports has been increasing, and that the trend may continue.

The results of all the above calculations are presented in table 1.11. The differences among the various combinations are truly remarkable. The annual remittance of physical resources varies from a low of 346 million MAPRALs to nearly 600 million (at 1986 prices). If we take only the amounts needed to service the debt we can see that the price decline since 1980 has meant that an additional volume of around 150 million tons of raw materials have to be produced and exported each year to compensate for such a decline. Obviously, the amount becomes much bigger if we consider total exports – close to 250 million tons. But these differences become even more striking if we look at the overall remittance during the repayment period. We can see here the influence of rising interest rates added to that of declining raw materials' prices. The combined effect of both variables results in a difference of 3 to 1 between assumption 1 (1986 prices) and assumption 2 (1980 prices). In absolute terms that difference means an additional outflow of over 9 billion MAPRALs. To have a clearer idea of what this means, let us take the case of one product: copper. Such extra outflow would represent for this metal an additional extraction, processing and export of some 50 million metric tons in just 23 years. This volume represents more than one-third of the estimated reserves of copper in Latin America (around 1975). Although the concept of reserves is quite flexible, as we shall see in a later chapter, an outflow of this magnitude would still represent a dangerous contraction of strategic stocks in a very short period. On the other hand, one should remember that each extra percentage point in the interest rate represents an additional outflow of 30 million MAPRALs (at 1986 prices). Hence, were interest rates to start

Table 1.11
Latin America: Amount of the physical remittance of the package of 18 basic commodities according to various hypotheses on export levels, repayment periods and interest rates
(in million tons of the package)

	1976–77	1980	1983	1985 (July)	1986 (May)
			At unit prices in:		
	$136	$217	$191	$172	$128[a]
A. Total debt ($400 billion)	2,940	1,843	2,094	2,326	3,125
B. Annual services ($45 billion)	331	207	235	262	351
C. Total annual exports[b] ($125 billion)	551	346	393	436	587
D. Overall remittance during debt repayment period:					
Assumption 1 (10% interest rate, 23 years)	12,890	8,137	9,263	10,282	13,820
Assumption 2 (6% interest rate, 13 years)	7,405	4,661	5,297	5,880	7,903

[a] Estimate.
[b] To cover debt services ($45 billion) and imports ($80 billion).
Source: Calculations by the author.

climbing again, this would add heavily to the already unbearable burden suffered by Latin America.

It is possible to infer, from what has been said above, that unless annual debt services are drastically curtailed, imports are severely restricted, and raw materials are adequately revalued, Latin American countries, and in general those of the Third World, will be condemned to the virtual plunder of their strategic resources. In a political dimension, this would mean a true territorial conquest of the South by the North, without any apparent military conflict or open bloodshed, but in the name of the sacrosanct concepts of 'development' and 'interdependence'. On the economic side, repercussions for Southern countries would be equally disastrous: along with the deterioration and exhaustion of the various resources that are basic to their subsistence – both renewable and non-renewable – production costs in real terms will inevitably tend to increase, notwithstanding technological advances that might be achieved. Expanding soil erosion and desertification turn farming into an almost impossible activity, which pushes rural populations to more fertile lands – which will eventually become deserts as well – or towards forested lands, which inevitably will be destroyed. The extraction and processing of minerals will be increasingly expensive, as the ores will be located at greater depths, with lower metal contents, and so on. That means that Latin American and other Third World nations will be exporting the cheaper fractions of those resources while keeping for future generations of their own citizens the poorest and costliest mineral strata.

On the ecological side, the damage will be irreparable: vast unreplaceable resources will disappear; what nature takes eons to build will be exhausted in just a few generations by the irresponsible behaviour of humankind. This is not valid only for minerals; it is valid as well for renewable resources. With each ton of beef or grain some amount of fertile soil also disappears. Forests vanish, and together with them valuable species of animal and vegetation.

It is possible that a portion of the raw materials that Third World countries have to export in order to service their debts goes to the strategic stockpiles of the US and other creditor nations (this happened in 1982, when the US advanced $1 billion to Mexico against oil deliveries for its strategic reserve). In such a case, those reserves would probably help to depress commodity prices in international markets, or, in the best of circumstances, to prevent 'inconvenient' price rises. This has been done on numerous occasions by the US government. We should not forget, in this respect, that low raw materials prices constitute one of the main anti-inflationary tools used by the US and other industrial nations. Even if those millions of tons of raw materials are not used for stockpiling, but are immediately consumed in the manufacturing of different goods, the metals will be there for recycling at the appropriate moment, and at least a fraction of them will be usable once more. It will be an inevitable fact, therefore, that resources will increase in the North and will decrease in the South.

As every society has to be sustained by a given material base, the above means that Latin America and other Southern regions are condemned to an inexorable impoverishment, which will weaken them and make them even more dependent. Large population groups will face fundamental and irreversible subsistence problems, much worse than those experienced by many nowadays. Although the conquest of the South by the North may not bring about large-scale bloodshed in traditional battlefields, many, many people will be dying in the cities and in the countryside, through malnutrition, diarrhoea and other infectious illnesses, and through sheer misery. They constitute those segments that always bear the burden of conquest, be it violent or silent.

It should be pointed out, however, that this scenario could be altered if the nature of plunder changes. Thus, if some initiatives to repay the debt with physical assets – land, factories, real estate, public and private corporate equity, among others – are adopted, then foreign trade might lose its importance in the outflow of resources, in comparison with what has been described above. However, in the longer term, the outflow of basic resources would be practically the same, if not higher, as the repatriation of profits and/or capital would require hard currency. That in turn would necessitate the export of physical goods. The quantitative difference between these two mechanisms of despoliation would derive mainly from the differences that might exist between interest rates and profit rates. But there would be a most important qualitative difference: in the second option, not only physical resources, but also the capacity to control important economic activities, would flow away. This would make the Latin American and other Third World countries even more dependent than they are now.*

* This may be the reason why the US is pushing so hard for stronger liberalization and privatization policies in debtor countries, a position that has been fully adopted by the IMF and the World Bank in the application of their own policies.

2 The Philosophy of Foreign Indebtedness and its Main International Agents

The philosophy of indebtedness

Nations borrow money abroad in order to cancel their deficits in current accounts, to expand or initiate new development projects and, in general, to supplement their internal savings deficiencies and to maintain or increase their international monetary reserves. Both government and private enterprise borrow as a temporary measure, in response to an unavoidable need at a given moment, thinking – very naively, of course – that such a need will cease to exist after a certain period of time. In the majority of cases it is assumed that such external loans will not only produce (through investments made with them) the foreign currency needed to repay the loans, but that they will also contribute to the self-sustained economic growth of the debtor countries, a process that will eventually make further borrowing unnecessary.

But reality has proved otherwise. Far from being a temporary phenomenon, foreign indebtedness has become a true addiction from which debtor nations have not been capable of escaping. As in the case of drug addiction, the doses become increasingly high. The causes are many and we have already examined a few of them. Firstly. the increasing cost of money, by causing annual debt services to absorb higher proportions of export earnings, led to additional borrowing, so that imports could continue after payment of services. Secondly, the very high economic growth rate policies applied by Latin American countries, while keeping intact their overall socio-economic frameworks, required a parallel increase in the import of all kinds of goods. Thirdly, the international banks followed aggressive strategies to dispose of their excess liquidity, transferring it to the avid Latin American markets. Fourthly, in the case of several Latin American countries with stable exchange rates, the considerable difference between domestic interest rates and the international ones made it very profitable to borrow dollars abroad, to convert them into Chilean or Mexican pesos and lend the resulting sums in Chile or Mexico, at rates which were substantially higher (in the case of Chile, for example, many lending firms were established in 1977-78 to carry out such operations, which, at certain moments, were yielding a rate differential of three or even four percentage points per month; of course, when the Chilean peso was devalued, after three years of stability, many of these firms went bankrupt). Fifthly, maintaining internal structures based on a high degree of economic concentration favoured the processes of 'dollarization', of importing superfluous goods and of capital flight; these processes were reinforced by acute inflation and, in some countries, by keeping overvalued national currencies. Sixthly, military regimes that favoured massive imports of armaments, which were generously financed with foreign loans, proliferated in Latin America. Seventhly, the claim was made that employment could be created through an expansion of the industrial base, and that the living standards of the majority of the population could be improved through the adequate provision of food, health, etc., without, however, modifying the basic structures of economic power and income distribution.

The basic premise underlying the indebtedness philosophy is that there must be a net transfer of resources from a lender to a borrower. For some economists it is only natural that developing nations request loans, since the abundance of savings *vis-à-vis* investment opportunities in industrial-ized countries contrasts with the opposite situation in developing nations, thus giving rise to a 'normal' flow of capital from the former to the latter.[6] But this 'normal' flow is in turn composed of two opposite flows, from which a net resource transfer must occur. Borrowers must remit resources to pay the interest and amortize the principal; as a result, new loans – bigger than previous ones – must be made available by the lenders, so that a net transfer is created in favour of the borrowers. This requires a continuous increase in the amounts disbursed and in the total outstanding debt. Dhonte, a well-known specialist in financial matters, says:

> Unless that increase proceeds at some minimum rate, not enough is left of new loans, after the old ones have been rolled over, to cover the interest payments, let alone to achieve a net transfer of resources. . . . Basic to an understanding of debt is the fact that its growth rather than its level is the crucial issue.[7]

This argument coincides with those of other economists who maintain that the only option available to the banks in order to avoid payments moratoria or straight default is to continue lending; at the same time, they insist that a moratorium is not a practical solution for developing nations, since they depend, almost totally, on the international banking system to manage their trade flows.[8] Nevertheless, the possibility of a moratorium is now being seriously considered in some quarters, especially since the collapse of commodity prices, in particular those of oil in early 1986.

For other economists, foreign lending plays a vital role in helping to alleviate the limitations in the supply of indispensable inputs for economic growth. If debtor nations apply 'proper' economic management, the moment will come, those economists argue, when these nations will be capable of sustaining a high growth rate without significantly higher additional foreign financial assistance.[9]

For 'developmentalist', 'liberal' or 'neo-liberal' economists, foreign indebtedness is something positive, intrinsic to economic growth. Thus, the majority of development models applied by Third World countries with mixed or market economies have relied on a permanent net transfer of financial resources from Western industrial nations (and Japan). These economists reject the notions set out by those who are against the use of foreign trade and indebtedness as the central instruments of the development process, arguing that such notions respond to political positions that reflect an anti-capitalist ideological bias. For example, Dhonte maintains that the position favouring indebtedness is of a 'technical' nature, whereas the opposite position is a 'political' one. He is of the opinion, therefore, that the 'economic' response to the determination of the optimum level of indebtedness corresponds to the 'technicians' and not to the 'politicians'.[10] In Latin America, the UN Economic Commission (ECLA) has maintained for years that a high rate of import growth constitutes a 'vital' element in sustaining economic growth policies, and that Latin American countries continue in sustaining strong external support in order to meet service payments. The ECLA argues that 'without economic growth social tensions become more acute, and the resistance to change, of those sectors that would have to yield, becomes greater.'[11] This is a most strange justification of the need for economic growth. It would seem to support a sort of bribing of the dominant classes so that they may 'yield', and thus not obstruct change. In other words: in order that those who possess the economic and political power might allow the 'trickle-down' theory to operate, to permit those below to get something they should be well paid in the form of an economic growth process, the best part of whose fruits would be allotted to them, as usual.

These and other similar arguments look like simple fallacies to us. Firstly, because it is not possible to separate the economic from the political, a fact that only the staunchest technocrats would deny. Secondly, because economic growth policies have not contributed effectively to the improvement in living conditions of the great majority of the Latin American population, and, consequently, the fact that they are so vital has not been proved. Thirdly, because a substantial portion of the capital that enters Latin America by way of development loans leaves through the back door and finishes up in private accounts in the US, Switzerland or the Bahamas. Fourthly, because not all the investments that are made with foreign loans are socially useful and profitable, they do not contribute to the self-sustained development of debtor nations. Fifthly, because there are strong reasons – not linked to a given economic or political position or ideology, but rather to the need to preserve the wealth of resources with which humankind is endowed, as well to the preservation of the human species in equitable and tolerable conditions – that point towards a policy of non-indebtedness and not towards those policies of financial dependence advocated by Dhonte and others.

Obviously, those who profit from the massive indebtedness of Third World countries are fervent supporters of the philosophy just explained. Private international banks, whose *raison d'être* lies precisely in the continuing and growing demand for credit, found themselves in this position for a long time, as their foreign operations were extremely profitable. According to Moffitt,[12] overseas earnings of the ten major US international private banks increased at an annual rate of over 33 per cent between 1970 and 1976, while those originating in domestic operations remained constant. As a result, the share of overseas operations in total earnings of those banks went up from 17.5 per cent in 1970 to 52.5 per cent in 1975 (recession years in the US) and to 46–48 per cent in the biennium 1980–1. It is estimated that US banks are holders of 37 per cent of the Latin American debt, with Japanese banks holding 20 per cent, British and German banks 12 per cent each, Canadian banks 8 per cent, French banks 5 per cent and other banks the remaining 6 per cent.

In the case of Mexico, for example, the share of private banks in total external financing has increased considerably, to the point that by 1984 only 19 per cent of its overall debt remained under fixed interest-rate clauses, while the other 81 per cent had been contracted at floating rates (40 per cent at the LIBOR rate and 41 per cent at the US prime rate). Quite some years back Green[13] had already drawn attention to the fact that the Mexican foreign debt had, since the mid 1960s, entered into an open phase of 'privatization, bankerization, and north-americanization', a process that was accentuated during the 1970s. As a consequence, while the public debt increased four-fold between 1970 and 1976, that of the private sector rose six-fold.

The massive increment in the overseas operations of private trans-national banks – producing huge earnings, as mentioned above – was an essential element, an inevitable factor we might say, in the process of salvaging the international financial system, that Latin American and other Third World countries undertook during the crisis following the first oil shock of 1973–74, which was felt in a very forceful manner during the recessive years 1974–76, but with effects that were noticeable until 1978. The Latin American nations, by maintaining or increasing their economic expansion rates during those years, contributed to the absorption of a large portion of the petrodollars that had accumulated in North-American and European banks, while at the same time absorbing vast amounts of surplus export goods from the same industrial nations, thus compensating for the decline in domestic demand in these same countries.

Dhonte confirms quite candidly this 'positive' role played by Third World indebtedness when he says:

> The accumulation of debt in recent years... was a response – *and an efficient one* – to the disruption of established trade patterns following the oil crisis and the 1975 recession. As it saved developing countries a brutal curtailment of their imports, it also allowed industrial countries *to offset a significant share of their oil deficit by a sizeable trade surplus with developing countries.*[14] (emphasis added)

Robert McNamara, former President of the World Bank, former US Secretary of Defense, and currently Chairman of the US Overseas Development Council, indicates:[15]

> The evidence that growth and progress in the developing countries now has a measurable impact on the economy of the United States reflects the importance of the developing countries to the United States as export markets and as customers of US commercial banks. . . . If the commercial banks of the OECD countries should now decide simply to roll over their loans to developing countries and do no further lending to those countries, not only would developing-country growth rates be sharply retarded, but the US itself *would lose some 20 billion dollars of its export sales to the developing world.* (emphasis added)

Other prominent North Americans also underline the very important role of Latin America in fostering the economic development of industrialized nations, and advocate a strengthening of ties between the US and its southern neighbours. It is worth quoting what A.F. Lowenthal, a senior US official with previous administrations, who has been closely associated with Latin American activities, says in this respect:[16]

> No U.S. Administration so far has seriously attempted to reform the structure of the international order *from which the United States has obviously gained so much*... Never has the U.S. Government seen a need to transform the nature of its relationship with Latin America... The financial bind that ties the U.S. so closely to Latin America is one example of Latin America's considerably increased significance for the world economy, and especially for that of the United states. Latin America's share of world industrial production and exports is growing. *So, even faster, is Latin America's role as a market for the manufactured exports of the more industrialized countries.* The continued growth of the developing nations, especially those of Latin America, *added a full percentage point to the aggregate growth rate of the more industrialized nations during the 1974–78 recession.* Latin America's expansion after 1973 certainly played a crucial role in recycling petrodollars and in contributing to continued export growth in the U.S. and other industrial countries. . . . Indeed, growth in the South... may be required to fuel the growth of northern economies in the years ahead. (emphasis added)

We are beginning to see more clearly the *deus ex machina* that fomented the monstrous foreign indebtedness of Third World countries during the 1970s.

The existence in several Latin American countries of military dictatorships which applied neo-liberal economic policies inspired by the 'Chicago School', stimulating the private sector, strengthening their commercial ties with the United States, and opening their markets to the inflow of North American products, was no doubt an important factor in the acceleration of the indebtedness process.

We could continue with other testimonies that are equally important, such as that offered by the Brandt Commission,[17] whose report also recognizes the vital role of Third World countries in absorbing excessive liquidity and surplus production of industrial countries, and postulates that the Third World should continue playing that role, in the name of so-called North–South Interdependence. Although the attempt is made to present this role as a leading one, in fact it is only that of a second-rate actor, a role for which the Latin American peoples have to pay a very high price in political, economic, and social terms.

Recent literature is rich in descriptive and analytical materials on the process of growing interdependence between Western industrial countries (plus Japan) and those of the Third World. In previous passages we were able to ascertain the importance that developing countries have acquired as markets for physical and financial surpluses owned, generated or handled by western industrial countries and Japan. The apparent complementarity in the relationship North-South does not entail, however, an equitable share in the benefits. On the contrary, being a relationship between unequal partners, the concept of interdependence resembles the peculiar vision of the boss *vis-à-vis* his subordinates. It may be true, as is often argued, that 'one part cannot exist without the other'; however, even if this is so, it does not mean that the present form of interrelationship is the only possible one.

It seems that there is a deliberate effort by those who deal with these subjects, both in the North and in the South, to present this growing interrelationship in a very favourable light, as if it were equally positive for both sides. In this book we attempt to demonstrate that the truth lies on the opposite side; that is, that such interdependence, both in the past and as it is being projected for the future, is actually a *harmful* process for Third World nations. The interdependence whose main operational instrument has been the international financial and trade system, has definitely favoured Northern interests, and will continue working in that direction, unless the basic rules governing the understanding between the strong and the weak partners are radically changed.

A very clear example of the way in which North–South interdependence works can be found in the industrialization process that has taken place in Southern countries. It is possible to observe, in an historical perspective, that the great leaps forward in Latin American industrial development have taken place when international financial markets have been closed or working under restricted conditions, and when communication channels, and hence trade, were impaired by some powerful upheaval. This was the case during the Great Depression, and, shortly after, during World War II. Thus, Latin America could start its industrial development between 1930 and 1945, based on its own resources. Conversely, when the international market situation goes back to 'normality', industrial development already achieved by developing nations begins to suffer the assault of international forces. Technological dependence is strengthened when local engineering and creativity, as well as domestic production of capital goods, are discouraged. Doors are opened to admit growing volumes of imported goods, and the incipient domestic industry is badly damaged or simply destroyed. Entrepreneurs turn their eyes, once more, to the 'central technological source', which promises high rates of profit. Governments, in turn, are dragged along, enchanted by the mermaid songs of multinational corporations, which succeed in penetrating the markets of less-developed countries and practically taking over their industrial development process. As from that moment, the economies of the North and the South begin to become intertwined and 'harmonized': interdependence has been consolidated.

When the road to a type of development based on self-reliance and creativity is abandoned, and the easier one based on foreign indebtedness and technological dependency is taken, then the internal savings capacity is discouraged and very serious distortions in investment and productive structures are introduced. Production of luxury goods for urban élites and exports is fostered, while production of foodstuffs and other basic consumer goods is discouraged. Besides, chronic indebtedness is perpetuated. Foreign debts show a continuous and self-sustained growth, which is completely outside the control of local authorities. According to Corm[18], creditor countries, through their own financial organizations and also through the international bodies where they have a predominant influence, do their best to control the economic and financial management of debtor nations. This can be clearly appreciated in the 'adjustment' policies imposed by the International Monetary Fund that are examined in the following section. We have to distinguish between the efforts of the US and European capital-exporting countries to gain control over debtor countries. The latter, due perhaps to the fact that only recently they lost their position as colonial powers, or because of their own subordinate situation with respect to the superpowers, show a less aggressively ambitious attitude towards Third World nations. The hegemonic power of the North/West uses isntead its food power, its money power (as main creditor), its trade power (as major market for Third World exports), and its military power (including its intelligence services), to try to modify political events in Southern countries, in order to accommodate them to the interests of its 'national security' doctrine. It also uses its undisputed strength within the two major multilateral financial organizations, the International Monetary Fund and the World Bank, to ensure that the policies designed and applied by these entities are closely in line with such interests. We shall now turn to the examination of these two international bodies.

The multilateral financial institutions

In view of the importance of multilateral financial institutions, it is pertinent to present a short account of their origins and performance during the 40 years since their establishment.

In 1944, delegates of 44 countries attended the Bretton Woods Conference, in the New Hampshire mountains in the United States, with the purpose of designing a post-war new economic order that would put an end to the depressions and economic upheavals that had characterized the previous three decades. To attain those objectives two institutions were created: the International Monetary Fund (IMF) and the International Bank for Reconstruction and Development (IBRD), better known today as the World Bank, designed to become the main economic organizations in a world free of economic disasters and wars. During the development of this conference the US played the central role since, by then, it had displaced Britain as the most powerful nation of the world.

The principal objective of the Bretton Woods agreements was that of maintaining exchange rate stability in order to stimulate the recovery of international trade. North American exports were being undermined by the monetary devaluations carried out by trade rivals and, in other cases, were completely displaced because of monetary or import controls. The intention was that of establishing new trade rules that would stimulate commercial exchanges of the most important countries, and, at the same time, invest a new international agency with sufficient authority to have those rules obeyed. Thus, the IMF was given the task of watching over the monetary stability and the trade practices of its members.

To avoid the reappearance of monetary conflicts among nations, a system called 'par value' was established, whereby a 'fixed but flexible' rate of exchange would prevail. It was agreed that competitive devaluations should be avoided in future, and the IMF was designated as the arbiter that would determine the appropriate rate-of-exchange levels. Each member would propose, after consultation with the IMF, a par value, expressed in gold, for its currency. Changes in the par value, after an initial 10 per cent free modification permitted only once, would have to be proposed by the country while its approval remained subject to the IMF decision.

The Bretton Woods agreements were intended to combine monetary stability and flexibility. By the end of the 19th Century, nations with the largest portion of international trade kept the value of their currencies fixed in parity with gold. Under the gold standard, the monetary mass was limited by the reserves of this metal possessed by each nation; this established a strict control over governmental spending and total money issued. The system made it very difficult for a given nation to maintain a trade deficit for a long period; countries had to export gold to correct their balance of payments shortcomings. Such adjustment of payments problems diminished, in turn, the money supply, causing deep economic depressions that gave rise to enormous unemployment rates. Because of its huge political and economic costs, the gold standard could not continue operating indefinitely. For that reason, with the occurrence of the Great Depression in the 1930s the system came to an end. The major trading countries devalued their currencies – something that had not been allowed under the gold standard – so that prices of their export products could become more competitive and economic recovery stimulated through the increase of their own share in international markets. At that time, poorer countries, including Asian and African colonies, lacking sufficient funds to meet their import needs, began to develop domestic industries so as to substitute those articles that previously had to be imported. Besides, those countries had established bilateral trade agreements whereby imports were paid for with earnings from their exports to the same countries.

The US and the UK, alarmed by the collapse of international trade and by the signs of increasing interdependence of Third World nations, realized that there was an urgent need to establish a new world financial order, open to their investments and trade and backed by monetary and financial stability. Such a new order, intended to maintain the vitality of the capitalist system, as well as its permanence and further development, is the one that came out of the Bretton Woods meeting.

One of the innovations brought about by the conference was that of providing member countries automatic access to credit, to allow those nations with balance of payments difficulties more time to recover, thus avoiding an economic depression. It was established that each member country should pay the IMF a contributory quota, the size of which was determined in accordance with each nation's national income, international trade and foreign reserves. One quarter of the quota would be paid in gold (the 'gold tranche') and the rest in the equivalent in national currencies. All this remains valid today.

The IMF, strictly speaking, does not lend money to its member nations; it sells them hard currency that is paid by members with their own currencies which are deposited with the IMF in the form of quotas. If the amount requested by a country does not exceed the value of its quota's 'gold tranche', the authorization of the foreign currency needed is almost automatic. An additional 25 per cent (the first 'tranche' of credit) is obtained without much difficulty. But each successive addition to that amount is conditional on increasingly harsh requirements.

The IMF controls an amount of nearly $90 billion expressed in terms of Special Drawing Rights (SDRs), an accounting currency created by the Fund, whose value is slightly higher than that of the US dollar. This sum, which is by no means modest, originates in the quotas furnished by member countries. By end-1983, however, member nations had made use of only 33.8 per cent of overall quota.* However, the IMF's immense power does not dwell here. The Fund is the cornerstone of a huge system, and its true importance lies in the authority that it has received from governments and financial institutions of the occidental world. None of the major credit sources of the developed capitalist world, be they private, governmental or multilateral institutions, grant credit to a country unless it agrees to comply

---

*Developing countries, in general, have utilized more than 100 per cent of their quotas, while industrialized nations have left theirs practically untouched. This explains the relatively low average coefficient of utilization.

with the requirements indicated by the Fund, which is considered the only safe guarantor.

When a nation faces payments difficulties and is in need of urgent financial assistance, the IMF sends a technical mission to advise government officials at the highest levels about measures that the government should adopt in order to be considered a worthy candidate for the requested credit. When both sides come to an agreement, an arrangement called 'stand–by' is negotiated, which consists of a credit line put by the Fund at the country's disposal, the delivery of which is conditional on the fulfilment of certain financial and economic objectives imposed by the Fund. Negotiations with the IMF are generally rough and difficult. Once concluded, the IMF's mission helps the government officials to draft a Letter of Intent, which spells out the actions to be undertaken by the Government in compliance with the promises made to the Fund. This Letter constitutes an essential requisite to obtain the economic assistance requested. Specific pledges concerning actions to be taken in various critical areas must be included, particularly in the foreign exchange area, import regulations, banking credit control, foreign investment policies, public expenditures, and others. It is well understood that whenever pledges contained in the Letter of Intent are not fulfilled, the right to use credits obtained under the stand–by arrangement are stopped. The complete IMF package of recommendations is generally called a stabilization programme because of its anti-inflationary emphasis. Although the IMF, formally and legally, has no power whatsoever to intervene in a country's domestic policies, in practice it does intervene whenever drawings are higher than the first credit tranche.

Even though details of each stabilization programme recommended by the Fund vary, the essentials of the economic policies that are considered convenient are always the same. Their basic components are the following:[19]

1. Abolition or liberalization of foreign exchange and import controls.
2. Devaluation of the exchange rate.
3. Domestic anti-inflationary programmes, including: (a) control of bank credit: higher interest rates and perhaps higher reserve requirements; (b) control of the government deficit: curbs on spending; increases in taxes and in prices charged by public enterprises; abolition of consumer subsidies; (c) the dismantling of price controls.
4. Greater hospitality to foreign investment.

The fundamental recommendations included in the stabilization programmes are in complete contradiction with the interest and well-being of the majorities in the nations concerned: in the first place, they provoke an immediate and strong economic contraction, affecting more severely those majority groups, without indicating how the recovery is to take place. Secondly, 'liberalization' of exchange controls and imports causes an even higher scarcity of foreign currencies by benefiting countries of the North through their increased exports to the South. The Fund's recommend-ations, therefore, cannot have as their real purpose the stimulation of autonomous economic development of Third World debtor countries, but invariably that of promoting private investment and international trade, which in fact only stimulate profits of rich countries, who are, precisely, the ones that dominate the IMF.

The total or partial dismantling of exchange and import controls, as imposed by the Fund, results in an increased demand for hard currencies (especially dollars, yen, Deutschmarks). This is offset by an increase in their prices through devaluation of weaker currencies, a measure that the Fund calls 'the establishment of a realistic rate of exchange'. However, the Fund does not seem to worry unduly about the extreme fluctuations that have taken place in the value of the dollar, which motivated, until very recently, a massive flight of capital from all over the world towards the US, with a number of additional economic disturbances in the other regions. Although the situation has turned around dramatically since mid-1985, it is still a valid assertion that the IMF does not interfere with US monetary and exchange policies, as it does with those of the Third World.

The Fund's activities are supposedly limited to the area of exchange rates and exchange restrictions. In practice, however, because trade policies are so closely linked to exchange policies, the Fund's authority spreads to 'restrictions due to balance of payments', which may bring about its intervention in import restrictions applied by governments, and even in measures of tariff protection that are sovereignly decided by each individual country. Hence, a stand-by agreement may include clauses that represent a virtual arrangement for trade liberalization. This is the key price of the Fund's assistance, although it implies other risks as well. On the one hand, liberalization may severely affect national industrial sectors, which require a certain degree of protection to face competition from Japan, the US or Europe. On the other hand, the Fund's help will probably promote imports of non-essential goods produced in industrialized nations. Although the IMF loves to preach austerity when promoting its stabilization programmes, those countries that follow the trade and investment promotion policies recommended by the Fund are in fact being stimulated to consume more than they produce and need, with the tragic consequences – reproduced *ad infinitum* – of balance of payment deficits, growing foreign debts, and the progressive pauperization of the majority of the population in debtor nations.

One of the things that most worry the Fund at the present crisis juncture is the sharp drop in imports of debtor countries since 1983, which has caused an equally sharp drop in the exports of creditor nations. This is the reason why the Fund is pressing the US and European private banks to increase lending to debtor nations that follow its recommendations. At the same time, it also presses borrower countries to liberalize their foreign trade and increase their imports – as soon as they increase their export earnings – instead of devoting such financial surpluses to the repayment of their debts. Take the case of Brazil. It was able to obtain substantial trade surpluses, of over \$10-12 billion, in 1984 and again in 1985. Worried that these monies might not be spent in an 'adequate' way, the Fund sent a high level mission to Brasilia in August 1984, to advise on the best course to follow. The recommendations of the Fund's mission were 'to burn dollars as quickly as possible and to restrict exports'. Shortly after this visit the Brazilian government adopted a package of measures designed to 'burn' dollars: the import of over 2,300 superfluous items (from toilet tissue to Michael Jackson posters) was allowed, and the amount of dollars that Brazilian tourists could take out of the country was trebled.[20] This situation has been drastically reversed since the new Administration took over in March 1985, putting an end to 21 years of military rule.

In the present circumstances of the Latin American crisis, the IMF's general prescription to diminish inflation at the expense of employment and wages, pressing down popular consumption, which is already quite low, only tends to exacerbate people's miserable situation besides slowing down economic growth. The Fund does not take into account the particular circumstances of each country. For instance, it does not make any distinction between those deficits that are caused by government policies, and those completely outside their control (e.g. US rates of interest). The burden of austerity measures tends to punish those groups that are most in need and least capable of paying its high social cost.[21]

Because of all this, the hostility of Latin American peoples towards the IMF has been growing together with the increase in their debts and the resulting economic and social stress. Some countries have declared open rebellion, as in the cases of Bolivia, Peru and, more recently, Brazil, although in each case in a different form (Peru, for instance, has established that it will not devote more than ten per cent of its export revenues to payment of commercial debt services; Brazil has declined to sign the classic IMF Letter of Intent, and refuses to put into practice the austerity measures suggested by the Fund). But the IMF's power is such that only very few governments dare to defy it in a frontal manner, as in practice it is almost impossible to get bank loans unless a previous agreement with the Fund has been signed. Argentina, for example, seemed to be marching towards confrontation, but finally gave in and is now on very good terms with the Fund, especially after the establishment of the 'Plan Austral', meant to eradicate inflation through a wage and price freeze (among other things). Since freezing was more effective in relation to wages than to prices, the Argentinian initiative was warmly received in Washington. The experiment seems to be losing its grip, though, as inflation in Argentina is accelerating once more.

The World Bank, which originally had a completely different objective – to lend money under specially favourable conditions in order to assist in the implementation of vast development programmes in Third World countries – has bent under the pressures of the US Administration and the IMF, and is now following very closely the orientation of its sister institution. In 1979 there was a drastic change in the bank's policies, to adapt them to the changing conditions in international financial markets. It transformed its line of 'global' and 'programme' loans – which were aimed at the financing of specific development programmes and projects – into a line of 'structural adjustment loans', the purpose of which was to help nations to overcome their current account deficits. This assistance is provided under three headings: (i) loans for immediate relief when there is a serious maladjustment in the balance of payments, thus permitting the afflicted nations to continue importing 'normally'; (ii) loans that facilitate export expansion, by helping to purchase abroad those inputs that are required by export activities; (iii) the loans are granted on condition that borrowing countries design a wide adjustment programme so that they can adapt their economies to the new international circumstances and conditions.[22]

Such structural adjustment loans stimulate tariff reduction and elimination of other trade barriers, the increase in public service tariffs to strengthen the financial position of state enterprises, the rationalization of fiscal subsidies, and the increase in domestic rates of interest to reach real levels that are similar to those in international markets. The bank, however, has not found it easy to impose this new category of loans, which so much resemble the IMF's stabilization programmes. According to the bank's own data, by end of fiscal year 1984 only 16 out of the 75 most active clients of the bank had negotiated 29 loans of this type for a total amount of $4,500 million.[23]

It is really difficult to swallow the concept of 'structural adjustment' as applied to the changes promoted by the World Bank. The term no longer has the meaning that the CEPAL (ECLA) 'structuralist' school of the 50s and 60s gave it: agrarian reform to change the very inequitable and inefficient land tenure systems; improvement in the terms of trade, to correct the inequalities in exchange processes at the international level; changes in power and income distribution systems within Latin American nations, to diminish the enormous social and economic differences recorded in these countries; elimination of the technological dependence and of the mono-exporting nature of these economies. These were the true 'structural' reforms needed by Latin American and other Third World countries, not those of trade liberalization and export promotion fostered by the World Bank and the IMF, with the enthusiastic support of the industrialized nations.

Policies and orientations of the Fund and the World Bank are basically determined by those countries that have most weight on their governing boards. The US, furnishing the largest proportion of the organizations' capital, did its best at Bretton Woods to ensure that the real power of decision be entrusted to the Board of Governors, in which the US Governor had, and still has, a veto. This is a privilege that the US has kept until today, which makes it impossible for Third World initiatives without previous US approval to have any chance whatsoever of being approved by these twin international credit organizations.

The responsibility of the US

We have already seen that an increasing portion of the Third World's external debt and of its annual services originates in the market increase in interest rates in the course of the last ten years. Although a well-known phenomenon, a brief summary of the reasons behind the augmentation in US rates is in order.

When Paul Volcker took over the Presidency at the Federal Reserve Board, in July 1979, the situation of the US economy was really chaotic. Since mid-1977 the dollar had been suffering the assault of wild speculative forces which, in less than five months, had pushed its value down by 20 per cent against the yen, 10 per cent against the Swiss franc, and 7 per cent against the Deutschmark. After some lukewarm measures adopted by the Carter Administration to defend the dollar, the US currency resumed its slide at the beginning of 1978. Dollar holders ran away towards other currencies and precious metals. By October 1978 the dollar had lost 67 per cent against the Swiss franc, 55 per cent against the yen, and 35 per cent against the Deutschmark. The non-interventionist attitude of monetary authorities allowed a further slippage. On 1 November, the Carter Administration announced the adoption of a package of measures to defend the dollar, its main element being the constitution of a $30 billion fund in foreign currencies to be used to purchase dollars. An austerity programme was also adopted – higher interest rates and lower rates of economic growth – which, however, risked plunging the economy into a recession. This did not occur but the success of the programme did not last either. By mid-1979 the dollar began to weaken once again and President Carter responded with a number of changes among the upper ranks of the financial areas within the Administration; the most important was the nomination of Paul Volcker. For a short time the downfall of the dollar was stopped. But by the end of September the price of gold, which had already jumped from $200 per ounce in early 1979 to $350 in June, having stabilized during the following two months, started a new upward movement which pushed the price to a level of $450 during the first days of October. Arab nations and other large dollar holders fled from this currency as fast as they could; it seemed that there was no limit to the dollar's collapse. On 6 October Volcker announced the adoption of new measures: the discount rate was increased one full percentage point, from 11 to 12 per cent, and additional controls were imposed on the monetary flow; however, they did not bring about the expected results. Inflation rocketed, together with prices of precious metals; the price index at the beginning of 1980 was moving up at an annual rate of 18–20 per cent. Two political events in November 1979 had conspired to make Volcker's measures fail: the taking of hostages at the Teheran US Embassy, and the problem of Afghanistan. The freezing of Iranian assets determined by the Carter Administration by mid–November frightened other Muslim countries and the flight from the dollar to gold and other precious metals became frantic (in the case of silver, hoarding and speculation by the Hunt family, the oil billionaires, was an additional factor in its price escalation). The price of gold got out of control, to reach $875 per ounce on 21 January 1980. Volcker then understood that the October measures were inadequate to stop the wave of panic that was buffeting international financial markets. Credit expansion had not diminished; on the contrary, it had stimulated speculation in precious metals and other commodities, notwithstanding the fact that the prime rate had passed the 20 per cent mark. For that reason, on March 14 1980, the Federal Reserve Board took the decision to impose direct credit controls, a measure that finally succeeded: metal prices went down very rapidly (by the end of March silver prices collapsed), inflationary and speculative tensions eased, and investors returned to the dollar, to take advantage of the higher interest rates being paid for deposits in this currency. From there on, except for short periods of erratic fluctuation, interest rates remained quite high and the dollar's value was substantially strengthened.[24]

When Ronald Reagan initiated his Administration in January 1981 and launched his famous economic programme based on the conjunction of three contradictory policies – increase in military expenditure, tax cuts, and budget balancing – even the most naive observer could anticipate that fiscal deficits, instead of disappearing, would tend to increase to unprecedented levels. So it happened. In only three years President Reagan demolished all existing records in this field. In fiscal year 1982–3 the deficit was nearly $200 billion, and remained at that figure (with minor fluctuations) during the following years. The US government must disburse over $100 billion in interest payments alone, that is about one-eighth its total budget; it is estimated that by 1989 this amount will go up to some $220 billion, equivalent to about one-sixth of the budget foreseen for that year. In other words, in order that the fiscal deficit *does not increase beyond its present level,* expenditure of around $120 billion should be eliminated, or taxes increased by that same amount. Even if something like this were to take place, the deficit would still remain at its present enormous magnitude, thus pressing capital markets. But, unless a dramatic change in policies takes place, the most likely event is that the deficit will approach the $300 billion mark by the end of this decade.* This means that it is unlikely that interest rates will drop significantly, although some temporary declines may occur. In fact, the prime rate declined by five percentage points between September 1984 (12.5 per cent) and September 1986 (7.5 per cent).

---

*In December 1985 the US Congress passed a law, known as Gramm–Rudman for its main proponents, that puts an automatic limit to the capacity of the Government for continuing indebtedness. According to its main provisions, the budget deficit should be gradually reduced so that in five years, by 1991, it should be zero. That is, the budget will be compulsorily balanced. Although promulgated, its constitutional validity has been questioned by some groups. At this date (1986) there is no assurance that the law will be implemented in its totality.

But many experts believe that the bottom has been reached and future movements will be upwards, particularly if foreign capital begins its return flight; this is precisely what Mr. Volcker fears, and the reason for his reluctance to promote a further decline in US interest rates. We shall come back to this point.

Thanks to the higher rates of interest, the value of the dollar *vis-à-vis* other currencies increased markedly, thus attracting vast amounts of foreign deposits into the US. This compensated for some time for the gigantic trade deficits that emerged because of the dollar's overvaluation (which reached its highest point during the first quarter of 1985), attaining the unprecedented levels of $120 billion in 1984 and close to $150 billion in 1985. Although the value of the dollar has diminished considerably since then, the trade gap is still running at the rate of over $160 billion a year. Such huge deficits, which arose as a consequence of steadily decreasing prices of foreign goods, prompting imports of almost everything, and the declining competitiveness of US exports, do not seem to be nearing an end, very closely resembling the fiscal deficits. This situation has led to a serious deterioration in many productive areas of the US economy, notwithstanding some protectionist measures so far adopted. Free-marketeers have obstructed almost any initiative to push US consumers back to domestic products; on the other hand, European and Japanese exporters have been able, so far, to continue competing on favourable terms even if their respective currencies have recorded substantial revaluations against the dollar.

It is important to note, however, that the Volcker measures were extremely successful in combating inflation, the rate of which has been kept at the low level of about 3.5 per cent per annum. But nominal interest rates did not follow the same course; as a result, real rates have increased very sharply, reaching a level of approximately eight per cent by end-1984, and six per cent by end-1985. Up to 1979 the real rate of interest used to hover between zero and two per cent, and sometimes it had even been negative. The present situation is therefore extremely beneficial to US banks and US savers. But for Latin American and other Third World countries the result has been disastrous, and to the increase in interest payments we have to add the sharp fall in commodity prices since 1980. Between 1980 and 1983 prices of copper, coffee, beef and wool went down by 30 per cent; those of lead declined by 56 per cent, sugar by 44 per cent, cocoa, bauxite, cotton, tin and iron by 20 per cent. In 1984 and 1985 the decline continued, although not in a uniform way, to the point that even the US media talk about a 'price collapse'. In 1986 oil joined ranks with tin and others (the notable exception being coffee) with a price slide that, in just a few weeks, dragged it to around $12 per barrel, that is half of what is was at end–1985.*

* The price of oil rebounded to about $15 per barrel in May 1986 due to the accident at the
Continued

The strangling pincer effect of the opposite trends in the cost of money and in the prices of raw materials is forcing a steady increase in the physical resource outflow from South to North. A truly infernal circle is created: defence expenses and fiscal deficits in the US go up, rates of interest increase (or do not decline sufficiently) and debtor countries are forced to augment their remittances of raw materials; at the same time, such export volume increases press commodity prices down, pushing debtor nations to further increase their exports and request additional loans, in order to meet their debt service obligations.

This effect is clearly seen in table 1.11: with an interest rate of six per cent and commodity prices at 1980 levels, total remittance of MAPRALs for debt repayment alone would be half the amount to be remitted under the assumption of a ten per cent interest rate and 1983 prices, and one-third if April 1986 prices were considered. The resulting differences of 2,700 or 5,000 million tons of important raw materials can be considered, therefore, as a forced 'gift' from Latin America to the North, particularly to the US. The concept of 'gift' (or more properly, of 'compulsory extraction') becomes even clearer if we ask what the Latin American nations are receiving in exchange for their excess remittances of oil, tin, sugar, copper, etc; the answer is: nothing! The services furnished when the loans were made had their price: let us say six per cent per annum; but the increase of this cost to ten per cent or more does not carry with it any additional service or benefit for debtor countries. So, the exchange is not only unequal, but monstrous! Furthermore, one could very well assume that the metals that Latin American countries have been, and still are, donating to the Reagan Administration are used by the US Government to manufacture the armaments employed against some of the Latin American nations themselves, and against other Third World countries. In any case, they are used to impose and maintain policies that, while in agreement with US economic, political, and military interests, are contrary to the true interests of Latin American nations and peoples. In other words, Latin American countries are donating the metals that serve to manufacture the chains that keep them tied to the yoke of the dominant Northern power.

Continued from page 41

Chernobyl nuclear plant in the Soviet Union, which is at least temporarily enhancing the prospects of fossil fuels for power generation. It remained at approximately that level, with minor fluctuations, for the remainder of 1986 thanks, to a large extent, to the agreement reached by OPEC to maintain and respect its production ceiling of around 17–18 million barrels per day. The OPEC Price Committee, at its November 1986 session, recommended the return to a system of fixed prices, with an initial target of $18 per barrel. A number of experts doubt, however, that OPEC is sufficiently strong to impose such a price increase in a buyers' market. On the other hand, the US Government might look with sympathy on OPEC's initiative, since it would help to alleviate the deep crisis affecting the US oil industry, which is also harming many US banks. In any case, it seems that the worst part of the oil crisis is over and that the oil market is heading towards stability.

Notwithstanding the purely illustrative character of the figures we have been examining – hence their lack of a very rigorous base – we believe they provide sufficiently clear evidence that the policies followed by the North, particularly by the US, have contributed decisively to accelerating the physical outflow from South to North. The conditions prevailing in financial and commercial international markets are forcing Latin American and other Third World countries to pay a forced tribute, in kind and in labour, of the magnitude shown above. In view of the terrible punishment that has been imposed on Third World countries, one could legitimately ask for the *n*th time: in the name of what or whom are such arbitrary cost-of-money rates or commodity prices fixed? How much longer will the future of nations and their populations be at the mercy of monopolies, of speculators, of the military–industrial complexes? We are certain, in advance, that the answer to such questions will be that these phenomena obey the 'laws of the market'. But we also know that such 'freedom of the market' exists only in the propaganda or in the naive economic textbooks that serve to train the leaders who will eventually manage the economy, enterprises and political life both of the North and of the South.

3 The Responsibility of the Debtors

We will now attempt to examine what debtor countries did with the borrowed money and why they borrowed so much in such a short period. It is not an easy task, because available statistics do not show the final destinations of what is brought into countries either as money or as goods, and there are many items that are not recorded at all. Of the nearly $400 billion of the total Latin American debt, how much was spent on armaments? How much on luxury and superfluous goods? How much on equipment to manufacture other luxury or superfluous goods locally? How much on goods that apparently are not luxury goods but are socially unnecessary? How much on equipment and technology to manufacture those goods? How much on travel abroad? How much flew away to be deposited or invested in Switzerland, the US, or other financial havens? These are some of the questions that an honest and deep investigation into the causes, mechanisms, and objectives of foreign indebtedness – and the consequent long-term mortgage and servitude of Latin American nations – should be in a position to answer.

In this chapter we will try to advance somewhat in this necessary process of clarification in conceptual and – when it has been possible – also in quantitative terms.

Once we have deducted that part of the debt that is attributable to the rise in interest rates and other financial charges, as well as to the decline in raw materials export prices (for detailed calculations on these, see chapter 5), a part that is not the direct responsibility of debtor nations, there still remains a portion, quite substantial, which certainly *is* the responsibility of these countries, of their governments, of their public and private enterprises, and of many of their individual citizens.

There is a component of marked irrationality in the behaviour of Latin American societies that impels them to live and develop in a manner that is not compatible with their means and resources, nor with their true needs. This component is closely associated with others of a multifaceted nature: immorality, naiveté, search for power and/or status, imitation of foreign lifestyles, developmentalist ideology, technological fetishism, free-market dogmatism, and so on. For obvious reasons, we shall not attempt to carry out a psycho–social examination of all the factors that explain social

44

behaviour, nor that of society's dominant or dominated groups, which give rise to phenomena such as the extreme exploitation of people and nature, consumerism, urban violence, or foreign indebtedness. Others have done this work – or might do it – better than the authors of this book. Our aim is mainly to try to understand the direction of some of the central forces that have pushed the Latin American development process along the route that it has taken, which has led the region to the present situation of extreme crisis and indebtedness, with all their nefarious sequels. Later on (see chapter 5) we attempt to wander, very timidly indeed, in the nebulous area of the forces that lead individuals to become consumers of the absurd.

In order to shed more light on the exploration of the labyrinthine caves of this craggy subject, we shall divide our analysis into two parts: the first, corresponding to capital flight under different disguises; the second, dealing with what we might term social waste: everything brought from abroad to produce and consume under the influence of irrational behaviour patterns.

The flight of capital

This is a wide category, which includes both capital flight to evade taxes, to hide income obtained through doubtful means, to buy real estate abroad, etc. and the capital that ought to have entered the Southern countries but never did, remaining abroad, as a result of fraudulent operations, illicit 'commissions' or other similar wanton tricks. Obviously, such items are not easy to identify or quantify, since their transit is mainly detected in the avenues of gossip; in national accounts or balance of payments data they appear with the elegant names of 'statistical discrepancies' and 'omissions or errors'. Those who possess a more precise knowledge of the twisted paths through which capital flies away, keep their secret very tightly. This is a swampy field, where it is risky to walk. Occasionally, however, authorized voices are heard which openly denounce the problem, and which permit us to visualize the scandalous magnitude reached by capital flight from Latin American nations. Such denunciations have become more frequent during the last couple of years, and have even become a favourite banner of the US Department of Treasury, to obstruct the lending process to Mexico and other nations, so as to force these nations to follow the dictates of US political and economic interests.

According to estimates gathered by *Time* Magazine,[25] the amount of capital flight from three Latin American countries, from 1979 until mid-1984, would have reached a figure of about $63 billion (28 billion from Mexico, 23 billion from Venezuela and 12 billion from Argentina). Reports published in Mexico[26] put the figure for the whole of Latin America at a level of $130 billion, which equals one-third of the total debt. According to data from the US Federal Reserve Board, more than one-third of the combined debt increment of Argentina, Brazil, Chile, Mexico and

Venezuela between 1974 and 1982, i.e. about $85 billion, was devoted to purchases of real estate and to making bank deposits abroad. Other estimates indicate that capital flight from Guatemala, El Salvador, and Honduras would, in recent years would have totalled $2 billion, while that attributed to Costa Rica would have reached over $350 million in just one year, 1981. It is also estimated that some $2.5 billion left Colombia in this way in only three years, while over $20 billion would have escaped from Venezuela since the oil boom of 1973–74. For other countries in South America the situation would be as follows: Peru, between $5 billion and $10 billion; Chile, around $8 billion; Brazil, between $15 billion and $20 billion; and in Argentina estimates vary considerably, from a low of $20 billion to a high of nearly $35 billion. But the highest performance in this field was achieved, perhaps, by Mexico. The former President of this country, José López Portillo, in his last message to Congress on 1 September 1982, indicated that no less than $42 billion had left Mexico in the previous few years, to be deposited abroad, to pay for houses and other property purchased by Mexicans. On that occasion the former President said:

> We do not know with certitude, but we have the information that recent banking accounts opened by Mexicans abroad amount to at least 14 thousand million dollars... Additionally, urban and rural real estate belonging to Mexicans have an estimated value of around 30 thousand million dollars. This has already provoked an outflow of foreign currency of some 8,500 million dollars, to cover initial payments... In consequence, we can conservatively assert that, in the last two or three years, at least 22 thousand million dollars have left the Mexican economy, while an unregistered private debt of around 20 thousand million dollars has been generated to pay for mortgages, a sum that has to be added to the foreign debt of the nation... I also have to add that Mexican investment in the United States during the last few years has been higher than the total foreign investment in Mexico throughout its whole history.

The data from various sources coincide therefore in showing that an amount which is roughly equivalent to one-third of the overall external debt of Latin America is quietly deposited in bank accounts abroad or invested in foreign real estate and other types of property, all of them belonging to a relatively small number of individuals, although the burden of this obviously falls on the shoulders of the remaining impoverished Latin Americans.

It will be argued that many of these operations were not of an illegal nature, since in Mexico and other nations there were no obstacles to the free movement of capital. It will also be argued that when a currency is as overvalued as the Mexican peso was until early 1982, it becomes clearly 'convenient' to purchase almost anything abroad. But what is convenient for an individual who has a financial surplus sufficiently large to have it invested abroad, is by no means convenient for the country. The assault on the various national currencies – which results from an unfortunate combination of poorly designed exchange policies and a profoundly inequitable income distribution – may not be illegal in a juridical sense but is profoundly immoral. A good portion of the money lent to these countries was money that originated in mercantile operations carried out on Mexican, Brazilian or Chilean soil, which was taken from its place of origin. The sheer magnitude of the numbers involved give an idea, at the same time, of the very high rate of profit recorded in industrial, commercial and financial activities in Latin America. Peasants, craftsmen, blue- or white-collar workers, are not among those who opened bank accounts or purchased real estate abroad. The economic 'miracles' mentioned earlier served, more than anything else, to fatten the foreign bank accounts of those who received 'benediction'.

The damaging effects of the speculative assault against the national Latin American currencies do not stop here. For purely psychological reasons, variations in the quotation of the dollar – either in the free, parallel or black market – sometimes quite sharp, tend to have a strong influence on the prices of all goods, including basic products for popular consumption, giving rise in this way to acute inflationary processes which, in turn, tend to intensify speculative currency transactions.

In a recent inteview with *Excelsior,* Antonio Ortiz Mena, former Secretary of Finance of Mexico, and currently the President of the Inter–American Development Bank, gave a somewhat different version of how much of the money borrowed by Mexico and other Latin American countries was squandered. Since Mr. Ortiz Mena knows so well the intricacies of the financial policies of his country and those of international politics, it is worth transcribing a few fragments of the interview:[27]

Journalist: *Sir, you say that, because during the last two six-year Administrations (sexenios) part of current expenditures were covered by foreign loans, we drew on future exports. In this case, are oil exports already mortgaged?*

Antonio Ortiz Mena: Sure, sure!

For how long?

If we take into account the magnitude of the foreign debt and the production of oil, and we calculate that the latter will be kept at the same level and that prices will remain stable, under such conditions it would take us 15 years to pay the foreign debt if present conditions do not change.

Does this mean that Mexico's economic development will stagnate?

It means that the money that we should have used to grow we are going to use to pay what we spent before, what we misspent . . . And we all have to pay.

It is better that those responsible for the crisis pay, or is it not?

No, they are not the only ones responsible. In other words: who took the money? It was not taken. It was consumed.

How was it consumed?

. . . if you spend the money, if you squander it, throw it away, and do not produce a thing with that money that you borrowed, then you are taxing future work. An example: the Underground (Metro) should cost around 20 pesos. The tariff is only one peso. Hence, each person that uses the Underground is receiving 19 pesos even if he does not know or does not need them, as is the case with rich people.*

Don Antonio, in relation to this subject of the foreign debt, many people talk about the fact that a large part of it has been generated by corruption. For instance, the Argentinians say that the military took away nearly $20 billion. The same thing is said about Mexico. What happened?

No, those are illusions. The quantities are of such magnitude that nobody can have them. Not one individual or group can have those quantities of money. The money was thrown away, was misspent on travel abroad, on the import of things that could be produced domestically.

Talking about Latin America, what part of the foreign debt was spent on armaments?

That is the other big item that has no payment source, and that is also taxing future exports. Many countries have debts because of armaments. Argentina, among them, spent a large part of what it borrowed in the purchase of armaments.

It is strange that people like Mr Ortiz Mena, with such vast experience in public affairs, can close their eyes to the existing evidence of the surreptitious outflow of so many billion dollars from the Latin American coffers, to benefit private groups or individuals, in just a few years. In the case of Argentina, mentioned by Mr Ortiz Mena *en passant,* there have been truly fraudulent operations in the handling of foreign loans, independently of what was misspent on armaments. According to declarations made by the General Public Prosecutor on Administrative Matters (Fiscal General de Investigaciones Administrativas) of the Argentine Government, published by *Excelsior* (31 May 1984) 'a large part of the huge foreign debt of Argentina originates in the fraudulent operations concocted with the international banks, especially of the United

---

*Mr Ortiz Mena is mistaken in choosing the example he gives. He mixes the inadequate utilization of foreign credit with the maintenance of subsidies to public services that might be used by people who do not need them. The investment made in Mexico City's Metro – which is utilized mainly by popular segments and not by the rich – cannot be considered an unwise investment. On the contrary, from a social point of view, it is a very wise investment. The subsidy problem is an entirely different issue, since it does not entail mortgaging the country abroad. Subsidies, as Mr. Ortiz Mena knows too well, simply constitute a transfer of resources from one social sector to another; from those who have more to those who have less. It is a way of redistributing income, which is sometimes badly applied. On the other hand, and in accordance with this question of subsidies, Mr Ortiz Mena himself, later in his interview, suggests that it would be convenient to apply a high petrol tax so that public transportation may be free. In that case, not even one peso would be paid to ride the Metro. (Late in 1986, however, public transport tariffs were adjusted upwards – with the metro ticket costing now 20 pesos – in compliance with the avowed official policy of curtailing most subsidies.)

States, by very high military officials, between 1976 and 1983'. Although it has not yet been possible to investigate all the frauds and illicit operations of that period, the General Prosecutor mentions several examples:

> Between July and November 1976 the Government of Argentina deposited in the Chase Manhattan Bank of New York over $22 million a month, for which the average interest rate received was five per cent. However, in the month of July of the same year, the Central Bank of Argentina renewed for 90 days a loan of $30 million granted by the same bank, at the rate of 8.75 per cent ... In May 1976 ... Argentina made deposits with the Banque du Crédit Lyonnais of France, and with the European–American Bank of New York, at interest rates of 5.75 per cent, while only a few days earlier the Central Bank of Argentina closed a deal with the Chase Manhattan Bank, whereby Argentina borrowed money at a rate of 8.5 per cent for 90 days; the same rate was paid by Argentina to the Bankers Trust of New York. A separate chapter must be devoted to the irregularities in the placing of the so-called 'Treasury bonds in foreign currencies', the investigation of which has not yet been undertaken in depth ... The frauds here are bigger than anyone can imagine, and each fraud leads to another fraud that is still worse.

It is evident that this kind of operation, generating high profits to lender banks and such damage to Argentina's finances, could not be the result of mere ignorance or the stupidity of those responsible for it; there must have been a very high degree of collusion between Central Bank authorities at that time and the executive officers of the US and European banks involved, who all benefited from these operations.

The surreptitious capital outflow is not limited to the cases mentioned above. There are other subtle ways to extract capital illegally from a country. For example, surcharges in import invoices and undercharges in export invoices are old tricks used frequently by commercial and industrial firms, both national and multinational, and even by officers of state enterprises, who thus leave abroad important amounts of capital that do not enter the Latin American countries; nor are they recorded; nor do they pay the corresponding taxes. In both cases the operation is carried out with a foreign firm as an accomplice, or with the headquarters in the case of a local branch. In the case of imports, prices appearing in the invoices are higher than those really agreed between the foreign seller and the local buyer. With the oversized invoice in hand, the buyer requests the corresponding amount of foreign currency or the necessary credit lines, with which the true value of the import is paid (a value that probably includes the 'commission' paid to the foreign partner), thus leaving a balance, generally quite substantial, to be deposited in the importer's bank account abroad. Over-invoicing also provokes an artificial increase in domestic prices, since it is the inflated value of the invoice that is taken to establish costs and final prices in domestic currencies, in the case of those products submitted to some kind of price control, as happens with many basic consumer goods in a number of countries. This type of 'elegant' swindle is detected quite often in the case of pharmaceutical products. Research carried out several years ago in various Latin American countries discovered that a common kind of fraud consisted of an exaggerated surcharge in the price of some basic drugs sent by the head office to its Latin American laboratories.

Under-invoicing, in turn, consists of the undervaluing of a given exported commodity, thus permitting the exporter to return to the national economy a lower amount of dollars, marks, or whatever currency, than was effectively received. This permits him to keep abroad significant quantities of hard currency. The Government of Costa Rica has estimated that under-invoicing in coffee exports represents an annual loss of nearly $50 million.[28] This fraudulent procedure is especially common where multiple exchange systems exist, since those quantities that have remained abroad could return to the country of origin to be converted into the local currency at the free, parallel or black market rates, which are usually much higher than the controlled ones, thus procuring a very high additional source of income for the exporter.

Another category of double-dealing, in which the immoral mixes with the absurd, covers the purchase of equipment that will never be utilized, at artificially inflated prices. In Brazil, for example, a number of such operations have been detected. According to information appearing in the journal *O Estado de São Paulo,*[29] several state enterprises of Brazil would have been 'induced' to spend over eight billion dollars in the acquisition of superfluous equipment. That payment was made, paradoxically, to avoid a default on the huge external debt, since Brazil had at its disposal one and a half dollars in credit for each dollar spent on such purchases. Thus, to close a hole, a much bigger one was opened! According to the same source, during the last three years the Brazilian external debt would have been 'fattened' by some $22 billion thanks to suppliers' credits. The Light and Energy Company of São Paulo, for example, was forced to acquire in France and Switzerland 30 large generators for a total value of one billion dollars, to be installed in three hydroelectrical plants that would never be built. Similarly, a new traffic control system was bought for $150 million in England, to be used in a new railway that does not belong to the government any more, and whose construction is paralysed. The system has been at the disposal of the Brazilian authorities since 1978, somewhere in London. In 1981, the Government of Brazil, attracted by favourable credit conditions, bought five Japanese ships for bulk transport, at a moment when the Brazilian shipyard industry, one of the five largest in the world, was working at 50 per cent of its capacity. The ships could not be utilized because they were technologically obsolete.

These and other similar cases give an idea of the dark side of foreign trade. It would be necessary to examine very carefully all the operations carried out by state and private enterprises during the last 15 years or so, to detect with more precision the magnitude of the frauds that have been committed, and to identify those responsible for them. Such a 'red chronicle' of the Latin American indebtedness process is essential to understand clearly the process of the wild, cancerous-like growth of this region's external debt which was not, as many tend to believe, or make others believe, the inevitable result of unalterable development dynamics. Behind the cold figures there is a long list of illicit and negligent acts that the people – who eventually pay the price – have the right and the obligation to know.

Waste: A result of social irrationality

This is the category which is most difficult to explain and measure, not only because the concept of 'rationality' itself can be interpreted in many different ways, but mainly because the cases, although detectable, are not easily measurable. To attempt some quantification we have to use value judgements, obviously subjective and therefore controversial, so that we can establish the limits between what we believe to be 'necessary' and what could be considered 'superfluous' or 'socially irrational'.

A first hypothesis is that a large portion of the external debt of Latin American countries derives from imports of non-essential goods, be they capital goods, intermediate or final goods. The production–consumption mode of the Latin American countries, by following a wasteful pattern in imitation of US or European lifestyles, is forcing Latin American societies to depend increasingly upon imported goods and technologies, thus leading to a situation of growing foreign indebtedness. The second hypothesis, which we shall examine in Chapter 4, is that this production–consumption pattern also accelerates the rate of progressive exhaustion of available resources and increases the degree of pollution and environmental deterioration, thus endangering the long-term viability of human societies themselves.

The model of wasteful consumption
The economy of industrialized capitalist nations and, to a lesser extent, that of socialist countries, is characterized by its high level of waste of energy and other basic resources. Once the essential needs of the entire population were covered – and this has been achieved to a large extent in all these countries – the urban–industrial development model required, particularly in capitalist nations, a high level of consumption diversification and the production of all kinds of goods for increasingly inter-connected markets. There are no imaginable limits to the invention of new goods, whose purpose is the satisfaction of 'needs' created by the same inventors. In the course of the present century Western societies have witnessed the explosion of massive and increasingly sophisticated consumption, and, together with it, or perhaps preceding it, a commercial–industrial development that has been dumping into the market higher and more varied quantities of such products. So that the merry-go-round of massive production might

continue gyrating at an ever increasing speed, two things were necessary: one, that the obsolescence process affecting all types of products be increasingly rapid; second, that the number of purchasers should also rise very quickly.

Obsolescence presents two main characteristics: one, that goods already available in the market be replaced by others that can show some new or improved feature; the second, that in case they are replaced by the same products, the replacement period must be shorter and shorter. Clothing has to be replaced when fashion leaders say so, not when it wears out. The same happens with cars and other goods. It has become a status symbol to change cars every year or two, or to acquire a personal computer, or to buy a perfume that costs $100 per ounce. What has been called the 'ingenuity' of US or Japanese technicians is nothing other than their ability to induce the premature obsolescence or uselessness of existing goods, as well as the imagination to invent 'needs' for new products.

The blessings of the highly-praised market competition, that has transformed the north-western economies into something like 'true cornucopia', are more apparent than real, because a large part of what comes out of such horns of abundance is nothing but waste. The economist Herman Daly rightly suggests that these unnecessary or noxious products be called 'bads' instead of 'goods'.[30]

The success of the system was based on the proliferation of innovations and the incorporation of growing strata of the population to the ranks of purchasers. When the domestic limits became too narrow, industrial countries went out to conquer new markets. For a long time trade between the metropolis and its colonies has been important not only for the raw materials necessary for industrial development it could extract from them, but also because it could place its surplus industrial products among the élites of those colonies. In modern times, with the advancement in communications, cinema, radio and television, tastes and fashions prevailing in countries of the North could be disseminated and thus penetrate with even more force into those of the South: first among the better-off urban classes and then among wider segments of the middle classes and the proletariat (cultural penetration among peasants has generally found more resistance). Although the obsolescence rhythm was somewhat slower, the adoption of new consumption patterns represented, anyway, the acceleration and widening of wastage, and affected the lifestyle of these societies deeply.

The penetration of new consumption and production modes did not everywhere follow a demonstrative and publicized route. There were other ways which, very effectively, changed traditional consumption habits and helped to open new markets for the colonial or neo-colonial powers' export surpluses. Consumption of wheat products by the indigenous population of Peru is one clear example. The staple grain in Peru used to be the quinoa, a very nutritious foodstuff that adapts quite well to ecological and climatic conditions in the high sierras. But US President Truman's Aid Programmes brought wheat to Peru and popularized consumption of wheat bread and other wheat products. Aid was soon followed by trade, with the result that Peru now has to import large quantities of this cereal, devoting to this purpose a sizeable proportion of its overall export earnings.

In other Latin American countries as well as in other Third World regions something similar has been taking place. In French Africa, for example, some commercial crops were imposed by force. Each town was forced by colonial authorities to farm a plot of cotton, or coffee, or groundnuts, or some other cash crop, the product of whose sales went to the coffers of the 'Commandant du Cercle' (Colonial Administrator). Compulsory farming intensified during the First and Second World Wars, as an African contribution to France's war efforts. The tax system implanted by colonial authorities also forced African peasants to abandon cultivation of subsistence crops in favour of the commercial ones. Cocoa in Ghana, groundnuts in Senegal and Gambia, coffee in Tanzania, and tea in Kenya are examples of how the use of arable land, and of labour forces that were available before for the production of food for local consumption, can be shifted towards the production of items of interest only to the colonial power. The deterioration of subsistence agriculture forced many African nations to import food from abroad to complement their domestic supply, even considering the very low per-capita consumption levels prevailing in those countries.

In the case of Senegal, for instance, its present dependence on imported food (which represents about one-third of total Senegalese imports) began with the expansion of groundnut cultivation. In order to induce the Senegalese peasant to sow and produce more groundnuts, at the expense of millet and other local food crops, the French Colonial Administration began importing large quantities of rice from French Indochina. Little by little the Senegalese cultivators increased their consumption of rice, which they bought with the produce of their groundnut sales. In less than 50 years the Senegalese diet changed completely, with rice displacing millet as the main basic food. Rice now represents about half of all imported food, and wheat – another product imposed by outsiders – represents a quarter.[31]

In Latin America the penetration of the production and consumption modes of the North was particularly fostered by the process of accelerated urbanization. Exposed to the constant bombardment of commercial publicity, urban middle classes quickly adopted consumption habits foreign to their traditional ones (in Chapter 5 we analyse this subject further). Industrial expansion, a kingpin of the economic development process in this region for the last 40 or 50 years, has been based on this widening of the market and on the growing sophistication of demand, as had happened before in the Northern countries. A central element in that expansion was the import of increasingly sophisticated technologies, used in the manufacture of increasingly complex products. Thus, a circular mechanism of industrial dependence on imports was established.

The history of the industrialization process in Latin America proves that the manufacturing sector has shown an increasing deficit in its external exchanges. Fajnzylber[32] demonstrates that the external deficit generated by the industrial sector in Latin America went up from $5 billion in 1955 to over $28 billion in 1975. Up to 1974 this growing deficit had been compensated by surpluses recorded in other branches of the economy; in 1975, however, the shortfall in the industrial sector alone became very large, giving rise to a total deficit of almost $10 billion in the overall balance of trade. Although industrial exports increased by a coefficient of 22 during that 20-year period, from $300 million to $6.5 billion, the increment in imports was around $30 billion. A recent Mexican study[33] reaches similar conclusions: various branches of industry progressively turned into the main importers of goods belonging to the same sector; moreover a backward trend in the degree of Mexican industrial integration was detected.

It can be affirmed, therefore, that the imports of the industrial sector have contributed most to the aggravation of the external economic problem of Latin America.

However, these characteristics are not exclusive to the present. More than 50 years ago Hobson had already noted that industrial economies have an intrinsic inclination towards excessive production and consumption:[34]

> This charge of materialism made against the more advanced industrial communities ... based on an over-stimulation of certain instincts for physical satisfaction, due to the innovating tendencies of modern capitalism with its elaborated apparatus of selling pressures ... leads to an excess which is due to a hasty exploitation of newly aroused tastes that absorb too much of human nature in economic processes. Getting and spending, we lay waste our powers.

Of course, the notion of waste as proof of social irrationality is not new. But its dramatic effects have not been as forcefully evident as they are nowadays. The vast expenditure of resources to meet the superfluous demands of certain population groups acquires a tragic connotation when consideration is given to the fact that there are numerous social groups that cannot reach a minimum level of satisfaction of their vital needs, especially food, health, housing, education, and clothing. We thus see how irrationality goes hand in hand with inequity. Conversely, we might say that the search for equity, for social justice, is homologous to the search for a higher degree of rationality in social behaviour. As we have indicated elsewhere,[35] rational derives from 'ratio' (reason), and 'ratio' also means the quotient between two numerical expressions. When a given mass of goods – for example foodstuffs or other essential products – is equitably distributed among the members of a community, that action is 'rational'; 'rations' are being given to each member of the community which are equitable, so that none of them may have to suffer any deficiency whatsoever in the satisfaction of his/her essential needs. When that mass of goods is limited, or relatively limited, the greater the reason to apply the criteria of 'ratio' and equity even more forcefully.

But classical, neoclassical, liberal, neoliberal economists, and in general all those who are in favour of the 'free market', consider that the true 'rationality' is that which stems from the free interplay of market forces, even if the result will not necessarily be the most equitable one. The distribution of individual quotas, that is the rationing, is effected by virtue of the strength that each individual can express in the market, a strength that is translated into his/her particular real purchasing power, and also by virtue of individual or familial consumption preferences. For these lines of thought this type of distribution model has the 'advantage' of not being 'deformed' by deliberate human interventions, particularly bureaucratic ones. The invisible hand will take care of allotment; if some people get less, it is because they have not worked enough or do not have the merits to obtain more. In any case, the market will give them the opportunity to rehabilitate themselves and to reach, perhaps even exceed, their welfare quotas. Besides, for these lines of thought, what is truly rational is the search for profit, since this is the kingpin of mercantile-capitalist systems. To manage an enterprise 'rationally' means, firstly, to select a workable programme of activities that will yield a profit, and, secondly, to select, among the set of acceptable programmes, the one which will maximize the enterprise's profits. It is understood that the working class should participate in these programmes, actively and enthusiastically. Godelier, who is very critical of this position, says:

> In a general way it is considered that the worker is 'rational' when he participates actively and totally in the functioning of the firm, thus making his the interest of the enterprise, which is to obtain the maximum profit . . . it is a complementary, derived and dependent rationality which the worker must possess, so that the rationality of the capitalist can be fully effective, and so that beyond the capitalist himself, the system may function without insurmountable contradictions.[36]

Others, however, are not at all convinced about the alleged advantages of the 'free market' system, since they believe there are visible hands that manipulate the market. For that reason it is preferable to leave the responsibility for an adequate distribution to other mechanisms that are not handled in obedience to private interests, but that, on the contrary, are operated by the base groups of the community, in their effort to achieve the maximum degree of rationality and social justice.

Distribution through the market, contrary to what is generally affirmed by its supporters, who consider it the most efficient method, generates a great deal of waste, through the excessive consumption and unproductive work typical of market operations. The problem is more serious than could be judged at first sight, because such waste not only provokes a diminution in the availability of resources required to meet the needs of those who, at present, lack the essentials, but also because it taxes, still more adversely, the quantity of resources that will be available for future generations. When we talk about equity we must take into account not only the present population of the world but the future generations as well. If we do this we will necessarily have to discuss the *limits* of today's collective consumption, even if adequately shared, so that the resources that will have to sustain those future generations are not exhausted prematurely. 'Rationality' implies, therefore, the attempt to achieve the satisfaction of the *real needs of everybody, today and tomorrow.* It also implies the avoidance of consumption and production methods that tend to cause ecological damage that will break the balance between the human species and its natural environment. The object is, therefore, to try to attain a situation of multidimensional equilibrium, through which non-exploitative relations, between human beings as well as between humankind and nature, will prevail.

There is a parallel between the present situation of indebtedness that afflicts so many Third World countries and the system of bonded labour by debt that existed throughout history in many parts of the world. Under such a system, an insolvent debtor could become a slave of his creditor, or be sold by the latter to a third party, as a result of the obligation assumed by the borrower to provide his personal services as a guarantee supporting the loan. The main characteristics of such an arrangement was that the value of the work provided by the debtor was not applied to amortize the principal. Furthermore, the creditor was not interested in collecting the principal; he was more interested in extracting the maximum possible work from his debtor, indefinitely, generation after generation; the death of the debtor, or of his descendants who inherited the obligation, did not put an end to the debt.

The present situation of Third World countries, and particularly those of Latin America, is very similar to that described above: a debt that is hereditary and inextinguishable. There is, however, an important difference concerning the origins and motivations of the debt. While slaves of past eras got into debt in order to survive, 'slave nations' of today get indebted, to a large extent, to acquire luxurious, useless, or non-essential goods, or machinery to manufacture them locally; these are commodities to satisfy the desires or just the whims of certain social groups. The addiction of those groups to sumptuous and wasteful lifestyles, in imitation of those prevailing in creditor countries, the 'Master' countries, have made them virtual cultural vassals of the North, while they remain oppressors – by their own will or by mandate – of other social groups, the economically and politically weaker groups, within the South itself. These latter groups, that constitute 'the South of the South', are the ones that, ultimately, will pay the costs of the conspicuous consumption, waste and plundering of the foreign overlords and of the domestic lesser nobility.

To better understand irrational social resource utilization and distribution, it is useful to refer to the categories devised by Paul A. Baran some 25 years ago to analyse the question of 'potential economic surplus'.[37]

In contrast to the concept of 'actual economic surplus' (which means 'the difference between society's actual output and its actual consumption'),

Baran presents the notion of 'potential economic surplus' which would be 'the difference between the output that could be produced in a given natural and technological environment with the help of employable productive resources, and what might be regarded as essential consumption'. Such 'potential surplus' is analysed by Baran under four headings: (i) what is lost through society's excess consumption by upper groups; (ii) the output that is lost to society through the existence of unproductive workers; (iii) the output lost because of the irrational and wasteful organization of the existing productive apparatus; (iv) the output forgone owing to the existence of unemployment, caused primarily by the anarchy of capitalist production and the deficiency of effective demand. Although there is no complete coincidence between what we understand to be 'social waste' and Baran's concept of 'potential economic surplus', it is still useful to look at these four categories.

(i) Excessive consumption: Although Baran strangely establishes two levels as yardsticks for the measurement of excessive consumption – one that is applicable to poorer countries, which he calls 'essential consumption', and another for richer countries which he denominates 'decent livelihood' – the relevant point concerning this categorization is that it establishes a limit between what is 'necessary' and what is 'superfluous'. Starting from this category, it is possible to establish the intimate relationship that exists between the overconsumption of some and the underconsumption of many. For the last two decades or so there have been discussions at the international level about the problem of 'basic needs', with the aim of finding adequate prescriptions that might help certain disadvantaged groups in different countries to solve the deficiencies they face in food and nutrition, health, housing, education, etc. But very little has been said about excessive consumption by other social groups, which is the other side of the same coin. We shall try to fill this gap, with some examples that show the irrationality of 'excessive consumption'.

In the most critical area of food and nutrition, we can observe in Latin America a number of cases of offensive excesses. From the underconsumption of food that is usual among the poorer half of the Latin American population, these societies pass to a situation of overconsumption by the top levels of the other half, which, it has been adequately proved, has deleterious effects on the health of the individuals forming those upper strata. It is well known that the human body, in order to function adequately, needs a certain daily intake of calories, proteins, vitamins, minerals and other elements. These quantities vary according, inter alia, to the age, sex, and physical activity of each individual. Once that threshold has been crossed, excessive food can cause a number of cardiovascular and other diseases.

Let us take, for instance, the case of Mexico, about which we have some very illustrative data. The average person in the ten per cent of the Mexican population with highest incomes consumed, towards the end of the 1970s, eight times more wheat products than the person in the poorest ten per cent, 11 times more meat, 17 times more dairy products, 5 times more vegetables, and so on. The result was that this person was not only eating several times more than one in the poorer groups, but was also exceeding by a large margin his/her nutritional requirements.[38] It is quite likely that today, seven or eight years later, because of the acute economic crisis affecting Mexican society, and the poorest groups most severely, such differences must have become more marked. All this means that, besides the useless expenditure of material resources involved in the production, transport, storage, processing, distribution and cooking of food that the human body does not need, we have to add the resources spent in the elaboration of medicines, in the building and maintenance of hospitals, pharmacies and medical schools, etc. that are devoted to curing hypertension, arteriosclerosis, diabetes, and other illnesses caused by food overconsumption. All those resources could have been utilized to satisfy the needs of those who are hungry or suffering from illnesses originating in underconsumption. We should, therefore, also charge to the account of irrational excessive food consumption the social cost of medical attention, etc. related to malnutrition and undernutrition, as well as the loss of productive capacity of the millions of undernourished adults. Obviously, we are not keeping account of the enormous social cost and the cost in terms of human suffering deriving from the loss of life of hundreds of thousands of children as well as from the miserable life of those who survive under such conditions.

To the above one should also add the waste of all the food which is thrown into the trash can, both as food leftovers and food that has rotted before it could be consumed by human beings or by domestic animals. The volume of this waste notoriously increases with income; it may reach astonishing figures. Studies carried out in Mexico City[39] show that more than 60,000 tons of bread and tortillas are lost each year in this way. From all metropolitan homes, overall food wastage of this kind would represent about 10 per cent of total food consumed. If we consider that total food consumption in Mexico City is of the order of 10 million tons a year,[40] the total loss of food in the capital, under that category, would amount to about one million tons a year, without considering industrial or restaurant food waste. This is an absurd amount if one thinks that it would cover a good fraction of the calorie deficiencies of the poorer half of the Mexican population.

Those mainly responsible for this kind of wastage are, as indicated, the higher income groups, who consume more and throw away more. The poorer segments, particularly those who still keep some of their ancestors' peasant traditions, use simple but effective methods to take the most advantage of the small quantities of food available to them. For instance, by cutting and cleaning those portions of the product that have become inedible through putrefaction, boiling the food for a longer period, adding sodium bicarbonate or herbs, or simply by grinding them and adding some condiment to eliminate or hide the bad taste the food might have, they can utilize perishable products that otherwise would go to the rubbish bin or to the dungheap. Besides, with what is really left over, they feed domestic animals such as poultry and pigs, that they may eat or sell to augment their incomes.

We do not know the figures for other Latin American countries, but assume that the behaviour of high-income urban groups must be quite similar. There are some patterns of conduct that do not recognize national boundaries.

(ii) Unproductive work: According to Baran's definition, unproductive work

> consists of all labor resulting in the output of goods and services the demand for which is attributable to the specific conditions and relationship of the capitalist system, and which would be absent in a rationally ordered society ... A good many of those unproductive workers are engaged in manufacturing armaments, luxury articles of all kinds, objects of conspicuous display and marks of social distinction. Others are government officials, members of the military establishment, clergymen, lawyers, tax evasion specialists, public relations experts, and so forth. Advertising agents, brokers, merchants, speculators, and the like.

All this wide spectrum of unproductive workers, although not directly linked to the production of essential goods and services, nevertheless sucks away a substantial portion of society's economic surplus. This characteristic is shared by other workers, such as scientists, physicians, artists, teachers and other similarly occupied people, who also 'live off the economic surplus but engage in labor the demand for which in a rationally ordered society, far from disappearing, would become multiplied and intensified to an unprecedented degree.'

This postulate represents, in our view, the heart of what is the irrationality of present development models in market-economy countries. While the essential needs of a large segment of the population in Third World countries are left unattended, the central economies, and also those in the periphery, dump into the market an increasing volume of useless and/or socially unnecessary goods. Status goods predominate over basic consumer goods. As we shall see, a substantial fraction of imports made by Latin American countries corresponds to the category of status goods, thus tending to aggravate the indebtedness problem.

We are not in a position to quantify the proportion of total Latin American output devoted to the production of these goods, but we are certain that it must be quite high. The internal logic of the prevailing development model has favoured those many subordinate or complementary activities linked to the processes of production and distribution of such goods. Such is the case of cars, which are often used as symbols of status goods.

The quantities of steel, rubber, petrol and other products that are used to transport one person by car are many times higher than those utilized to transport the same person by bus, tram or train. Similarly, the amount of energy, iron, tin, paper, etc. that is used to produce, process, and distribute one kilogram of canned fruit is several times higher than that utilized in the production and distribution of the fresh product. The quantities of materials of all kinds that go into the construction and furnishing of a 1,000 cubic metre luxury house, that will probably lodge not more than six or seven individuals (including domestic service), are many times higher than those utilized in the construction of a more modest house of, say, 80 or 100 cubic metres, which will also provide shelter to the same number of people. The differences in the amounts of bricks, cement, pipes, steel, timber, copper, etc. can be truly staggering, without even counting the luxurious ornaments added to the mansion. The same argument can be applied to an almost infinite number of cases.

Consumption patterns in Latin America (as in other parts of the world) have been changing alongside the acceleration of the urbanization process and growing incomes. In the area of food one notices the incorporation into the diet of a larger number of industrialized foods and the increase in consumption of animal products, all of which generally utilize a much higher quantity of energy and other resources per unit of nutrient supplied.

We shall again take an example of what happens in this respect in the food sector in Mexico, although the illustration is equally valid for other Latin American countries. According to estimates based on data from the National Survey of Income-Expenditure carried out in 1977 at the home level, and also from the National Nutrition Institute of Mexico, a high correlation can be found between increasing incomes and the level of nutrients supplied by animal products. While in the 10 per cent lowest-income group animal products furnish only 6 per cent of total calorie and protein intake, a figure that is considered to be extremely low by many nutritionists, in the upper 10 per cent of the population the proportion becomes 26 per cent for calories, and 48 per cent for proteins, the latter considered to be excessively high. There is a noticeable trend towards the adoption of a North American food consumption model which includes plenty of milk, meat and eggs, and also a large number of industrialized products: canned, precooked, frozen, dehydrated, etc. Cereals at breakfast, dehydrated soups, potato chips, pop-corn, packaged pastry, and so forth, are consumed in increasingly large quantities. The case of industrial, packaged pastry is very illustrative. It is produced in Mexico only by two major firms, Bimbo and Continental. It is estimated that their output was increasing, until very recently, at a rate that was four times that of demographic growth, according to studies carried out by the National Institute for the Consumer in 1978. This gives an idea of the equally expanding consumption of these products, poor in proteins but rich in sugar and saturated fats, which are harmful to health. At the time of that study a gram of protein in such pastry was costing 15 times that of the protein contained in normal bread. If we add to such pseudo-foodstuffs all the other sweet and salty products, plus soft and alcoholic beverages, we find a consumption scheme that is highly irrational, from both a nutritional and an economic point of view. It should be borne in mind that, according to the income-expenditure survey mentioned above, the poorer groups devoted about 12 to 15 per cent of their total food bill to the purchase of this kind of article, while at the same time they showed – and continue to show – important nutritional deficiencies. Overwhelming publicity has thus been able to penetrate into the most disadvantaged groups of the urban population.

A special mention must be made, within this category of food waste, of the increasing consumption of other industrialized products such as canned, dehydrated, and frozen foods. They constitute the base of a prosperous agro-industrial activity that today is the real motor of agricultural development. Agriculture has become the less important element in the agri-business equation; not only has the participation of the primary sector in total agro-industrial GNP diminished, but the most important decisions affecting agriculture, and the population living off it, are taken outside its realm, in offices that are located, in the majority of cases, in the US or Europe. It is true that a certain degree of processing is needed to permit many foodstuffs to be ingested by human beings. It is also true that such transformation helps the conservation of perishable products, and their long-distance transport. But such industrialized food products not only supply areas that are distant from production sites, but compete with fresh produce even where this is readily available without noxious additives. Moreover, agro-industries often compete with the final consumers in the procurement of different products, which are a source of profit for the former and vital food for the latter, thus affecting prices of the fresh product. Although theoretically such competition might be seen as convenient for the primary sector, in practice its effects, when positive, do not always reach the primary producer, particularly if this is a small producer who has to meet very severe delivery conditions set up by the industrial plants that purchase their produce. This situation is aggravated by the enormous dispersion of small producers, who become the victims of an intricate net of middlemen, acting on their own or on behalf of processing plants, wholesalers or large supermarket chains. Small producers, who are also consumers, usually sell at low prices and buy at high prices whatever they need. Their bargaining power is weak, not only with respect to the buyers of their generally meagre surpluses, but also with respect to the stores or places where they have to acquire the things they need both to live and to produce. Terms of trade for peasants and small farmers are extremely unfavourable, and are progressively deteriorating with the advancement of commercial agriculture and agro-business: a result of the changes in the composition of domestic and external demand.

Still in the agricultural area, we must mention a very special category of waste. We refer to the application of production techniques that, with the object of increasing yields, tend to degrade soils and other natural resources. 'Modern' agriculture, which is very capital-intensive, not only uses high quantities of energy, pesticides, fertilizers and other inputs, but it gradually 'eats' the base resources of soils and water which sustain it. Reports from the US show that the layer of humus in such a typical agricultural state as Iowa is being reduced at the rate of ten tons per acre every year; this means that a farmer working sloping lands loses about two bushels of corn per bushel produced.[41] Not long ago, *Time* magazine[42] published an article about the gradual exhaustion of the main water-tables that supply the water used by six major agricultural states in the mid-west and south-west of the US. According to it, those water reserves will be practically depleted around the year 2030; this means that in about 50 years that fertile region will return to the 'dust bowl' that Steinbeck described with such drama in his *Grapes of Wrath*. A recent study by the Worldwatch Institute, a well-known research institution specializing in demographic and food problems, reported that some 25 billion tons of humus are being lost every year all over the world; this will inevitably lead to the appearance of hunger pockets in different areas of the planet, as well as to an increase in the price of food crops. Studies carried out in the corn belt of the US show that for each inch of vegetable cover lost, yields decrease by 6 per cent. The US, the Soviet Union, India, China, and many other countries face this problem,[43] which is discussed further in Chapter 4.

On the same line of thought we can consider as a special type of waste all those products that are exported to satisfy needs or wishes of consumers in richer countries – including the needs and wishes of their pets – thus subtracting them from domestic availability. This is particularly true of meat or cattle exports to the US that, directly or indirectly, end in the belly of those millions of cats and dogs that are found in New York and other cities. This is a most disgusting aberration, since there are millions of Mexicans and Central American citizens who seldom, if ever, eat meat.

All labour utilized in the production of the non-essential goods exemplified above and of many other equally unnecessary non-food items, can be considered unproductive from a social point of view. If we add the necessary labour to produce, transport, and process the physical resources employed, we arrive at an enormous amount of labour virtually lost, and at an equally huge wastage of physical resources. A given function can be performed in many ways, but the one generally chosen is not the simplest, the most direct, the one requiring less resources of any origin and imported components. The 'modernization' of central and peripheral economies has brought with it a remarkable increase in this type of waste. Moreover, as such waste contributes to the growth of GNP it is hailed as an evident measure of 'progress'. In many cases the illusion is created that 'modern' products are cheaper, because their monetary value has been artificially compressed through payment of lower prices for the raw materials acquired from Third World countries, or for the labour used to extract and process such materials, or for the energy utilized. But real waste is there: human and physical resources that are employed in unnecessary tasks, when they could be better employed in activities geared to satisfying the essential needs of the deprived part of the population.

If modern societies were rationally ordered, it is likely that a sizable part of the goods and services currently produced would become redundant, as indicated by Baran. Even admitting the huge difficulties that exist in defining a socially satisfactory and acceptable demarcation line, we believe that it should not be very hard for a given community to distinguish between necessary and redundant articles. What may be more complicated is the task of disentangling the present web in order to weave it in a different way. In other words, when a 'rationally ordered society' stops producing certain goods and services that are deemed unnecessary or useless, that society will have to find some use for the redundant labour force, in activities that are linked to the well-being of *all* members of the community. As has already been indicated, in the nations of the Periphery there are still many people who do not get enough food, who lack shelter, clothing, health services, recreation, and access to culture. All or most of the present unproductive work could be utilized in such socially useful output while at the same time occupying the *entire* active population and not only a part as is the case today. If there happens to be an excess of available labour over and above what is necessary, the surplus could then be exchanged for free time *for all*. Each community could decide, in a more autonomous way, how it uses its labour force.

But the main problem in relation to this new way of weaving the web centres around those workers 'captive' in well-paid activities that will have to disappear. Blue- and white-collar workers in, for example, armaments factories and corporations – which have become a major factor for economic growth in countries such as Brazil and Argentina – or in luxury-car plants, or in toxic pesticide plants, or in agro-industries that produce junk food, will not look kindly on any attempt at social reorganization that aims to eliminate waste. They will probably become allies of those entrepreneurs whose businesses are menaced by social transformation. To the extent that such an alliance – which brings only illusory benefits to the workers – can be broken, to the same extent will it be possible to disentangle the web without breaking the thread.

It is possible that in a 'rationally ordered society' total labour expenditure in the output of goods will be lower than present levels, since consumption will be adjusted to social needs and not to the false and sometimes extravagant needs invented by the market. Whether this will be the case depends on how labour is distributed today between essential and non-essential goods, and on the amount of unsatisfied essential needs of lower income groups. In any case, along with adjustments in the structure and composition of consumption, which will lead to the greater importance of cultural and spiritual needs, there will be a marked increase in employment in these kinds of activities, as was rightly indicated by Baran. At the same time, the valuation of human work will also have to change, in relation to the new priorities and social objectives. For vast masses of workers who, after hard toil, earn barely a minimum subsistence wage (explicit or implicit, as in the case of peasants and small farmers), there should be a significant revaluation of their productive efforts. It would be necessary to devalue or eliminate parasitic activities invented to oil the capitalist engine.

We could well ask, in this respect, what is the social utility of activities linked to the financial–mercantile–speculative sector – expanding vigorously during the last 25 years or so – and why it is that they are so well paid. Stock exchange brokers, investment advisers, financial middlemen, commodity and currency traders, specialists in futures, options, etc., have transformed world economic activity into a huge gambling house, the Grand Casino of the World. These experts in the financial game can help in the speculation with almost anything: farm products, metals, oil, currencies, information, etc. We do not know how many 'experts' of this type exist, but whatever their number, they must be sucking up a sizable fraction of the overall economic surplus. Another even more important fraction is taken by the speculators themselves. We should reiterate, therefore, that such activities are not only superfluous in the sense that they do not add anything positive to the circulation process, but they are harmful, since they tend to favour market instability, particularly in the case of raw materials. They also make the process of exchange more expensive (somebody pays for the succulent earnings of the numerous agents and their employees), and ultimately, damage Third World raw materials producers, especially the smaller ones. We believe the time has come for an exhaustive investigation of the activities of this vast financial sector, in order that its true role can be examined. How much does it cost the international community? Who pays for that cost, and what could be saved from that activity for the sake of rationally ordering Third World societies?

One could visualize a society in which, at least in some areas, organized producers could relate *directly* to equally organized consumers, so that they could *jointly* decide what to produce, how much, and what should be paid for the various production factors. Because a 'rationally ordered society' would be of a much simpler nature, such direct understanding would certainly be easier to achieve.

(iii) Irrational organization of production: This category of waste refers to the output lost because of the irrational and wasteful organization of the existing productive apparatus. Essentially it deals with the existence of idle capacity in plants and installations, resulting in unproductive investment. For Baran it is an aberration that, even in prosperous years, some productive plant should remain idle, even in booming industries. At first sight, this might appear totally correct; however, it is only partially so if we examine it in the light of the two previous categories. In fact, it is possible, rather probable, that a substantial portion of idle industrial capacity is equipment for manufacturing non–essential or noxious goods; such

equipment may not be modified for the production of socially needed goods. If that is the case, its non-utilization would be a positive step, since its utilization would only mean an increase in the volume of waste; to the initial waste constituted by the construction of plants devoted to the output of useless goods, one would have to add the further waste resulting from their functioning. In a situation of rational ordering it would be preferable to leave those plants idle, limiting the loss to their initial installation. Moreover, it will perhaps be necessary to *provoke* the closure of plants that produce socially unnecessary goods.

The case of those plants that produce, or could produce, essential articles, and that are idle, is entirely different. The same applies to agricultural lands that are kept out of production either deliberately, or because of negligence or lack of interest, as is the case with many *latifundia* in Latin America. In both situations there is a real waste, often stimulated by monopolistic production structures which work at a lower capacity in order to keep up prices and profit rates. We should insist, anyway, that the traditional criterion of return maximization should not be utilized without considering the composition and destination of the product.

In this category what is truly relevant is the frequent inadequate planning in the use of equipment and installations for producing and handling essential goods. This results in high physical losses along the productive and distributive processes, in the various phases of primary production, transport, storage, transformation, and marketing. This is particularly true of perishable foods, where very high losses are usually recorded. In the primary production stage, besides losses originating in climatic disturbances, substantial losses can occur due to defects in human actions, such as, for instance, the lack of timely fertilizer application, or the lack of sufficient credit allowances to purchase the required inputs, or the inadequacy of techniques applied. In the post–harvest phases important losses are also recorded, both in quantity and quality, due to faulty handling and packing procedures, lack of sufficient and adequate storage facilities, including cold–storage installations, insufficient and deficient distribution facilities, and so forth. Estimates of these types of losses in some Latin American countries fluctuate between 15 and 25 per cent, with a much higher proportion still in the case of perishable products.

We do not have data on physical losses in other productive branches that can be attributed to deficient planning and use of equipment. We may assume, however, that such losses must be much smaller than in the agricultural sector. In any case, this is a matter that should be investigated.

What is worth stressing is the dualism of the criteria employed by capitalist entrepreneurs. Since they have to compete among themselves – particularly in the more advanced market economies – they try their best to improve productivity, so as to decrease costs and avoid waste of resources. But this is done, obviously, to maintain or increase profit rates, not in the spirit of diminishing or eliminating the waste of social resources. Manufacturers of superfluous articles who apply strict productivity norms are in fact economizing on a certain amount of resources; however, they are anyway wasting social resources to increase the supply of useless goods. This is a subtle contradiction of capitalistic systems that should be analysed and brought into the open, so that wasteful activities should not be allowed to continue hiding behind a facade of 'high productivity'.

In a rationally ordered society the question of plant localization and size will have to receive great attention. It is likely that simplifying the production of essential goods will permit a better use of human and natural resources available at the local level, thus facilitating industrial deconcentration, with many benefits for present conurbations. Such a thing would help to avoid or alleviate the social waste represented, inter alia, by the unnecessary stress suffered by millions of workers, and by the time and effort lost in transport to and from work.

According to recent information, about one-third of Japanese workers – who are considered amongst the most efficient and productive in the world – suffer from nervous and mental disorders caused by stress, which, in turn, derives from a rigid working discipline and the intense desire to excel and not to make mistakes. Similarly, a recent study by the National Institute of Mental Health in the US reveals that about one-fifth of the adult US population suffers from mental disorders, in particular anxiety, schizophrenia, and the use of alcohol and drugs.[44] This is probably the result of tensions of a hyperindustrialized society, almost wholly urbanized and extremely competitive.

In very large conurbations it is usual that workers spend several hours a day travelling to and from work. In Mexico, for instance, it is not unusual for a worker to travel around three hours in the morning, and another three in the evening, using a mixture of several means of collective transport. His actual working day is, therefore, 14 hours or more.

(iv) Unemployment: This category comprises the loss of potential output caused by the unemployment of human resources, mainly because of deficiency in effective demand. Baran illustrates his case with figures which, assigning to the unemployed a notional productivity that is equal to the national average, show the magnitude of the forgone output. 'No one can estimate the benefits to society that might have been realized, if the energy, the ability to work, the creative genius of the millions of unemployed had been harnessed for productive ends'. It is difficult, we think, to disagree with this basic postulate (with the probable exception of those who support 'Reaganomics', 'Thatchernomics' or 'Pinochetnomics'). It is necessary, however, to examine carefully the concept of 'productive ends' appearing at the end of the quoted sentence. We assume that such ends must be understood as related to essential consumption; otherwise, there would be room for contradiction with the first two categories of waste. But Baran's position concerning this point is not at all clear.

Although Baran says that the 'optimum' of production and consumption may not necessarily coincide with the 'maximum' output that might be obtained in a given period, as a consequence, for example, of the shortening of the working day or the elimination from production of poisonous substances, he maintains, on the other hand, that optimizing the handling of resources in a socialist economy does not entail the limitation of consumption to what is essential. On the contrary, he says 'it can and will go together with a level of consumption that is considerably higher than what the criterion of essentiality might suggest.' This seems to us to be totally in contradiction with what he states earlier when talking about the subject of 'essentiality' within the context of a 'rationally ordered society', and it brings us once more to the key issue of the borderlines between what is essential and what is superfluous, what is fair and just and what is excessive, between what is rational and what is irrational. One could understand Baran's position as a gesture to show that socialism does not condemn society to mere subsistence livelihood, and that it can offer, if it so wishes, as good or even better fruits than the capitalist system. But the trap is precisely here: if we jump outside the limits of 'essentiality' – even admitting that this concept may be defined broadly, to include not only the bare essentials but also some other things that have become of common use – we may easily fall into one of the wagons of the capitalist train, which travels in one direction only: that of excessive consumption, of waste, of irrational destruction of nature. The train's course cannot be changed; to do so would mean to run off the capitalist system's rails, whose laws impel it toward the constant expansion of production, and therefore of consumption.

But the locomotive of the European socialist countries is also running in the same direction; although more slowly, it is also pursuing seemingly unlimited material improvement in order to compete with Western nations. This position could have been considered just and reasonable after World War II, when both East and West European peoples were facing the challenge of recovering their lost levels of welfare. Those levels have already been reached and widely surpassed; the European socialist societies have been able to satisfy generously the essential needs of their populations. It is not clear, therefore, why they should continue following the same trail. Not being ruled by the principle of individual profit, they should also be searching for the fullest possible harmony with their natural environment.

It seems undeniable that socialist societies do not commit the consumerist excesses recorded by Western capitalist societies (although it is debatable whether this is because of their convictions or for lack of opportunity); it also seems true that in a centrally planned economy it should be easier to apply the brakes to environmental degradation, or to wanton destruction of natural resouces. However, so that socialism can reach the indispensable objective of natural harmony, in practice and not only in theory, it is imperative to reaffirm the criterion of essentiality as the central element in the economic and social functioning of socialist societies.

This has become even more valid since the People's Republic of China is entering into a phase of expanded consumption of electric appliances for the home and other similar articles which, if a very rigorous criterion of essentiality were to be applied, might be considered as not strictly necessary. According to recent information,[45] a remarkable increase in the output of electric washing machines, fans, refrigerators, colour television sets, clothing, photographic cameras, tape recorders, etc. has taken place in response to the growing demand of the Chinese population. It seems that the objective of the People's Government is to quadruple both industrial output and per capita income by the year 2000. Given the demographic dimensions involved, a consumption and production expansion of the size foreseen – without discussing its intrinsic merits – will result in a gigantic increment in natural resources' utilization; if this is not carried out with proper ecological considerations in mind, China might face environmental upheavals that are similar to those experienced by countries that have already passed through the stage of initial mass industrialization.

At this juncture we turn once more to the central problem, which is the definition of what is essential and what is superfluous. Is an electric refrigerator essential or superfluous? Or is the excessive capacity of the artifact superfluous, over and above the minimum needs of the family? Or is the single–home refrigerator superfluous whereas the collective one might be considered essential? We could also ask whether it would be entirely fair – in the name of ecological rationality (an abstract concept for many people) – to consider as superfluous a number of electrical machines and tools that are designed to alleviate domestic burdens, especially those of women, or that will permit the adequate conservation of food in hot climates, or make conditions of life more bearable in extreme climatic conditions, or allow isolated communities, or for that matter people in general, a better cultural connection with the rest of the nation or the world. The great challenge of the Chinese and other Third World people is how to reconcile these demands with the need to preserve their resources as well as their economic independence. The reply might be found perhaps in the local development of appropriate technologies, that permit the economy of resources per unit of the goods produced, and at the same time do not depend on imported technologies or materials, do not require foreign borrowing, and are amenable to small, communally owned and managed enterprises.

If the dilemma is serious enough in socialist countries and in much of the Third World, it is more so in countries of the First World. For those in Western societies who can still remember how conditions were before the arrival of electricity to their homes, and with it 'the comforts of modern life', the return to more primitive and sterner forms of life is not likely to be accepted, even if that meant a less rapid destruction of natural resources. Robert Caro, in his book on the life of US President Johnson,[46] describes how conditions were in Hill Country (his birthplace), a very poor rural area in Texas, in 1937, before electricity arrived in that remote region. To fetch water and boil it constituted a very heavy workload. Water had to be brought in buckets from distant rivers or wells; for a family of five that meant the transportation of 300 tons of water and walking some 2,500 kilometres each year. But as water had to be boiled, farm women also had to bring wood for fuel and constantly feed the oven with it. During summer months, with temperatures of over 30°C, heat in the kitchen became unbearable. The stove had to be kept constantly hot, because it was used not only to cook but also to make bread, to can fruit and vegetables (which had to be processed the same day they were ripe, otherwise they rotted). As there was no refrigerator to keep the food, each meal had to be made separately. Besides, laundry had to be washed in hot water, and then ironed, which was the hardest part of all. Irons were very heavy; they were made of 'true' iron, which burnt the hands all the time. During harvest time it was necessary to cook for 20 or 30 people, besides helping in the shearing and the picking. Even if sick, women had to keep standing, always busy in the various activities described. It is highly doubtful, therefore, that women in Hill Country, Texas, or in so many other similar places, would be willing to go back to those times.

The question, however, is whether the modernization process is going too far. Nowadays, Hill Country and other peoples are also using all kinds of electronic gadgets to over-ease their domestic work and entertain themselves. Is an electric shoe-shiner an indispensable tool? Or a personal computer? Or a microwave oven? In the case of many Third World rural or urban areas, where the situation is much worse than in 1937 Hill Country (no clean water, very little food to cook or can) it should be very clear where the priorities for improving living conditions lie. Even admitting the necessity to alleviate heavy human toil by means of machines or tools, we must also think about the massive investment required in sanitation, housing, drinking water provision, food production and distribution, and so on. These are not incompatible, of course. But a serious incompatibility could soon emerge if the list of labour-saving devices becomes too long.

Evidently, it will be up to each society to determine what it considers essential or superfluous, what is lacking and what is in excess, and adopt remedial measures to eliminate both the deficiences and the excesses. The location of the borderline between essential and superfluous stops being a merely economic issue, as it exists too on the cultural and economic planes. The perceptions of those in power of the dangers of overconsumption and wasted production, and the general disposition towards adjusting present consumption patterns, will ultimately determine where those limits will be placed. For the purpose of our study, and more concretely in relation to the waste recorded in Latin America through imports, we have assumed, for purely illustrative purposes only, some simple criteria and made equally simple calculations, as shown in the following section. We believe it would be important to refine such procedures in order to undertake a more detailed and in-depth effort to quantify social waste. This, of course, necessitates a definition of limits. Starting from the import side, it might first be determined what and how much could be suppressed or substituted. Then we could continue with a wider examination of the overall production and consumption structure in each nation. The journey towards a rationally ordered society requires a much deeper knowledge about the present functioning of the numerous cells in the social fabric, and their interrelationships.

Waste via imports

Production and consumption of socially non-essential goods pose severe demands on the external sector, since many of those goods require imported components and parts, besides the capital goods needed to manufacture them locally; in addition, the more extravagant manifestations of conspicuous consumption are satisfied with imports of luxury finished goods.

In order to estimate the impact of clearly 'superfluous' goods (including goods that can be dispensed with or that can be produced locally) on the development of the indebtedness process of Latin America, we have examined the foreign trade statistics of Brazil, Chile and Mexico, three of the major debtor nations in the region, between 1978 and 1981, a period purposely selected because of its high import growth rates and unprecedented import levels, combined with a very rapid expansion of the external debt. Such statistics are presented with a degree of disaggregation that is sufficient to detect the more visible cases of superfluity, but insufficient to identify superfluous destinations of goods that might appear to be useful and that are included in wider categories of raw materials or finished products. For this reason we had to make a number of assumptions which, we believe, err more on the side of caution than on that of exaggeration.

The criteria used (arbitrary but not lacking in logic) to define the superfluity of certain categories of goods were the following.
1. Some items such as beverages and tobacco, perfumes and cosmetics, office machines, TV sets, clothing, photographic and cinematographic materials, watches and music equipment, were deemed to be wholly unnecessary, be it because of their uselessness, dispensability, or be it because they were amenable to substitution by domestic production; we applied, therefore, a 100 per cent discount to these items. In those cases where we found direct information on the import of cars, as was the case with Chile, we also applied a discount of 100 per cent. It is likely that within each of such sub-categories there are objects that were indeed necessary and that could not be manufactured locally; however, not being able to identify those cases, we have compensated for that possibly excessive deduction with a more moderate discount in other categories.
2. From the remainder of the item denominated 'manufactures, various,' (once all those sub-categories already discounted under (1.) had been deducted) we considered one-fifth as 'superfluous'.
3. We judged one-third of what was imported under the item 'parts for automotive vehicles' to be unnecessary, assuming that such a proportion

corresponds to cars and the other two-thirds to trucks, buses and other transport vehicles that are socially useful.

4. We discounted 50 per cent of the item appearing under 'special transactions and merchandise not classified under any item' whose lack of specificity might indicate that the item includes many dispensable articles. It is probable that this item (No. 931 under the Standard International Trade Classification) includes armaments, notwithstanding the fact that these come under another number. In none of the countries whose statistics we examined did we find any transaction whatsoever under item 951, which is the one covering armament imports. This is very strange, particularly in the case of Chile, a country that imported nearly $700 million worth of armaments in the period 1977–1980, according to specialized UN sources. In any case, this is a subject that should be thoroughly investigated.

5. In the case of imports of raw materials, fuels, chemical products, basic manufactures, machinery and transport equipment (minus those items already deducted) we applied a 10 per cent discount; this discount is, in our view, very conservative; if the criteria of essentiality were to be applied more rigorously, that percentage would have to be increased, since there are many products and machines that are imported to manufacture, transport and distribute socially unnecessary or useless goods.

6. In the food item we did not apply any discount, although – as indicated above – a rather substantial part of imported foodstuffs is wasted in excessive or superfluous consumption.

We are aware of the rudimentary and subjective nature of the criteria utilized. We wish to insist, nevertheless, that the main objective of our argument is not to condemn this or that good or service, nor to achieve a high degree of arithmetrical accuracy, but rather to draw attention to the need to adopt some essentiality criteria that can guide the foreign trade policies of the Latin American countries, in order to eliminate – as far as possible – all those things that are socially dispensable and thus avoid an unnecessary drain on resources.

The quantitative results of this exercise are contained in tables 3.1 to 3.8 which are grouped at the end of this chapter. In the case of Mexico, the import waste thus calculated reaches a figure of some $14 billion for the period 1978–81, a sum which represents roughly one-sixth of the accumulated foreign debt in 1981. For Brazil, the corresponding figure is about $10 billion, one-ninth of its debt three years ago, although the main cause for the overall increase in its total import bill was the augmentation in oil prices. Chile constitutes the most pathetic case, with an estimated import waste figure of approximately $5 billion, more than one quarter of its debt in 1981. The detailed figures published by the Central Bank of Chile (not by any opposition group) are very telling: imports of luxury or dispensable goods, such as TV sets, cars, clothing, perfumes and cosmetics, alcoholic beverages, tobacco and toys, among others, reached scandalous proportions in the four years under review. In 1979, for example, more was spent on the import of whisky than on that of agricultural machinery; in

1981 imports of cars amounted to over $420 million; i.e. equivalent to one-third of all capital goods imported, for a country with a total population of 11 million.

The contrast between waste of resources via imports in Latin America and, for example, in the Indian subcontinent is truly striking. With its GNP at a level between those of Brazil and Mexico, India's external debt is about one-fifth of that of the other two countries. If we apply to India the same criteria used in the Latin American cases, we reach a figure of around $4 billion, much lower than those estimated for Mexico, Brazil and even Chile. In per capita terms the contrast is extremely sharp: $6 in India, nearly $80 in Brazil, $200 in Mexico and over $500 in Chile.

If we added to the above figures the enormous amounts spent by Latin American tourists in the purchase of all kinds of luxury goods, we would arrive at much higher wastage values. In the years of the economic boom, hundreds of thousands of Brazilians, Argentinians, Mexicans, Chileans, Costa Ricans, and so on travelled to the US, to Europe and other places, to enjoy themselves and to fill their luggage with electronic objects, clothing and other similar items, of which no records remain in official import statistics. Although it is difficult to assess the true magnitude of the tourist monetary outflow, there is no doubt that it contributed substantially to the increase of the total foreign debt. The fact that Mexico, Brazil and other Latin American countries obtain important amounts of hard currency via tourism does not justify Latin American waste through the same channel.

We consider it pertinent to compare the situation of Latin American countries with that of India because that comparison helps us to understand that the Latin American indebtedness was not an inevitable process. India had to face the same conditions in international financial markets, but could escape from the temptations of excess liquidity and thus be capable of establishing and sustaining a more autonomous development model. India is the fifteenth most important industrial producer in the world; it possesses a highly developed capital-goods industry, including steel, machine tools, and other technologically sophisticated products, both for domestic consumption and for export. This country exports technology through its own multinational firms and has become self-sufficient in food. It has technical and scientific cadres of the highest level. At the same time, however, 50 per cent of its population is below the poverty line, and 70 per cent of its total labour force works in agricultural activities, a situation not very different from the turn of the century. Urbanization, industrialization and the expansion of trade have not modified these basic parameters, although they have not pushed the country into a high dependency situation or into excessive foreign indebtedness, as in the case of Latin American nations.

Another aspect of the great differences between India and Latin-America – which may explain to a certain extent the tiny imported component in Indian consumption – is the very low level of commercial publicity that one finds in India. According to reliable estimates[47] total advertising expenditure in India is close to $0.37 (US) per person, whereas the corresponding figure in Mexico is 30 times higher: about $11 per person.*

We believe it would be highly desirable that Latin American nations and international institutions investigated in more detail the development and consumption policies applied in India so as to gather the central elements that permitted this nation to achieve such a highly autonomous growth and development process.

Waste via militarism

The most irrational and noxious form of waste is that constituted by the manufacture, trade and consumption (final utilization) of military equipment. Obviously, the accumulation of armaments is less harmful when it is limited to its first two phases, but history shows that, sooner or later, many of the arms that are produced and sold are finally utilized. At present the 'nuclear ghost' is limiting the consumption phase to conventional weapons in conflicts that are geographically restricted – weapons that, however, have an increasingly destructive power.

Third World participation in arms waste is mainly found in the non-nuclear area. This participation has been growing rapidly; according to specialized UN sources,[48] military expenditures of developing nations have increased more rapidly than those of developed countries, as shown in table 3.9. Between 1970 and 1980 total military expenditure by the latter grew by about 10 per cent, while that of the developing nations grew by 65 per cent; thus, they absorbed in 1980 around one quarter of total world expenditure on armaments. At the same time, the growing militarization of the Third World meant that a higher proportion of its GNP originated in the military sector, a proportion which in 1980 exceeded that corresponding in the developed nations.

East Asia was the Third World region with the highest military expenditure in 1980, followed by West Asia; it is likely, however, that the relative proportions have changed since 1980 due to Iran–Iraq and other Middle East wars. Latin America appears with a relatively small amount of some $7 billion in 1980. These official figures, which probably underestimate real military expenditure, nevertheless constitute an inordinate amount for a region that does not appear to have any serious

---

*The real difference must be much higher, since Indian figures include expenses in public campaigns, such as those in favour of the Society against Cancer and many others, whereas those of Mexico correspond exclusively to commercial propaganda. The figure for Mexico was calculated by the author on the basis of information obtained from the National Consumers Institute, according to which total expenditure on TV commercials in the capital reached in 1983 83 billion pesos, a sum equivalent to some $550 million at the exchange rate of that time. Since this figure represents roughly 70 per cent of all national publicity expenditure, the overall figure would have been around $800 million or $11 per capita.

conflict among its nations, and where so many live under very precarious conditions. It seems that a large proportion of the armaments, besides providing satisfaction to the respective Armed Forces in each country, are used mainly to repress internal dissent, which is triggered precisely by the enormous material deficiencies suffered by a large part of the population.

Although part of the armaments acquired by the military establishments in several of the Latin American countries is domestically produced, with Brazil, Argentina, and more recently Chile, becoming significant exporters, Latin American nations import increasing quantities of military equipment and arms of various types. It is estimated that such imports grew more than 300 per cent between 1969 and 1978 (in constant dollars), with Argentina, Brazil, Chile and Peru being the most important purchasers (Cuba is another sizable importer of arms, but we do not have precise data on its acquisitions). During the period 1977–80 these four countries imported over $3 billion worth of armaments, with Peru in first place with nearly $1 billion worth in the four-year period.

A material expression of the waste deriving from the military expenditure – apart from the loss of lives and human suffering resulting from the transformation of such expenditure into effective utilization – is constituted by the employment of physical resources. The specialized UN source mentioned above indicates that in 1980 a significant proportion of certain minerals were used for military purposes. Thus, in the case of aluminium, nickel, tin, and zinc, the proportion was over six per cent; in the case of lead it was eight per cent and that of copper, eleven per cent. The case of oil is even more illustrative: almost a half of all the oil consumed by developing countries (excluding China) can be attributed to military uses. This confirms our earlier point that a 10 per cent discount on imported manufactures and fuels was conservative indeed.

It is not our purpose to examine in detail the economic, political or moral aspects of the arms race in the various countries and regions of the world, not only because this would go beyond the scope of the present book, but also because this is a subject that has been dealt with extensively by many organizations and individuals around the world. We believe, however, that we could not avoid mentioning, albeit very briefly, some significant figures that confirm the degree of irrationality reached by modern societies that devote so much of their energy and creativity, of their human, physical, financial and scientific resources to the production, marketing and utilization of destructive and deadly instruments. What is worse, as mentioned previously, is that the military industry constitutes today a fundamental pillar in the socio-economic schemes of developed countries, and of many developing nations as well, involving vast segments of their workers – manual and intellectual. The conversion of the military industry into a peace industry – ploughs instead of guns, homes and schools instead of barracks – will have to be one of the central elements in the process of transforming present societies into the rationally ordered ones we have been talking about.

Table 3.1
Mexico: Imports of goods ($ million)

Item	1978	1979	1980	1981	(1978)	(1979)	(1980)	(1981)
Foodstuffs and live animals	563	576	2,161	2,089				
Beverages and tobacco	23	43	67	67				
Raw materials (excl. fuels)	762	668	894	1,185				
Mineral fuels	263	251	292	348				
Animal and vegetable fats and oils	73	84	157	118				
Chemical products	1,052	1,000	1,384	1,513				
Basic manufactures	1,408	1,416	2,353	2,870				
Machinery and transport equipment	3,510	4,650	6,622	8,787				
Agricultural machinery					56	290	341	340
Office machines					113	124	220	235
Television sets					—	96	173	237
Vehicles					1,037	1,313	1,764	2,151
Vehicle parts					775	1,073	1,500	1,822
Manufactures, miscellaneous:	393	662	934	1,319				
Clothing					42	113	174	295
Photographic and cinematographic materials					35	29	62	61
Watches					32	46	57	70
Musical instruments					32	48+	76+	96+
Special transactions and other merchandise not specified by kind	—	2,563	3,560	4,653				
Total	8,053	12,502	19,431	24,193				

+Estimated

Source: UN, *International Trade Yearbook*, 1981.

Table 3.2
Brazil: Imports of goods ($ million)

Item	1978	1979	1980	1981	(1978)	(1979)	(1980)	(1981)
Foodstuffs and live animals	1,405	2,080	2,140	1,776				
Raw materials (excl. fuels)	492	708	855	830				
Mineral fuels	4,937	7,314	10,749	12,159				
Animal and vegtable fats and oils	59	142	105	43				
Chemical Products	2,187	2,812	3,461	2,269				
Basic manufactures	1,496	1,824	2,162	2,030				
Machinery and transport equipment:	3,907	4,213	4,860	4,435				
Office machines					173	191	190	206
Vehicles					165	168	206	197
Vehicles parts					142	155	188	182
Manufactures, miscellaneous:	477	595	587	510				
Photographic equipment, not specified					44	68	45	36
Photographic and cinematographic materials					63	87	86	95
Watches					47	51	52	39
Musical instruments					45	64	62	54
Total	15,016	19,731	24,949	24,072				

Source: UN, *International Trade Yearbook*, 1981

Chile: Imports of goods ($ million)

Item	1978	1979	1980	(1978)	(1979)	(1980)
Non-food consumption goods of which:	463.7	682.4	1,070.1			
Pharmaceutical and medicine				42.4	46.9	58.8
Tools				21.0	29.7	37.6
Cars				41.7	118.1	202.5
TVs				66.0	61.4	69.5
Radios				36.2	46.8	65.3
Domestic electrical equipment				19.2	45.3	67.7
Clothing				28.3	38.0	87.6
Shoes for common use				4.9	10.4	26.2
Toys				11.9	17.8	28.4
Photographic products				6.6	11.6	21.0
Perfumes and toilet articles				10.0	16.3	23.6
Books and periodicals				11.5	15.3	20.7
Bicycles				8.8	9.4	8.4
Other				155.2	215.3	352.8
Consumers goods of which:	441.6	517.4	966.2			
Whisky				8.2	13.9	13.6
Intermediate goods of which:	1,443.8	2,138.8	2,565.2			
Tobacco, raw				7.3	8.8	15.2
Spare parts and assembly parts				78.4	106.6	119.4
Capital goods of which:	653.3	879.1	1,219.0			
Computers				20.1	24.5	40.4
Telecommunications equipment				13.9	29.1	33.5
Office machines				13.3	16.8	24.6
Total	3,002.4	4,217.7	5,820.5			

Source: Central Bank of Chile, *Balance of Payments – Chile*, 1980

Table 3.4
Chile: Registered imports, 1980–1981 ($ million)

Item	1980	1981	(1980)	(1981)
Consumption goods of which:	1,226.4	1,907.2		
Cars			202.7	427.6
Capital goods	984.9	1,249.7		
Intermediate goods of which:	2,912.4	3,206.9		
spare parts and assembly parts			171.7	185.5
Total registered imports	*5,123.7*	*6,363.8*		

Source: Central Bank of Chile, *Economic and Social Indicators 1960–1982.*

Table 3.5
Chile: Imports of luxury, dispensable and replaceable goods ($ million)

Item	1978	1979	1980	1981
TVs	66.0	61.4	69.5	
Radios	36.2	46.8	65.3	
Domestic electrical equipment	19.2	45.3	67.7	
Clothing and shoes	33.2	48.4	113.8	
Toys and sports equipment†	20.9	26.4	33.7	
Photographic products	6.6	11.6	21.0	
Perfumes and toilet articles	10.0	16.3	23.6	
Bicycles	8.8	9.4	8.4	
Whisky	8.2	13.9	13.6	
Raw tobacco	7.3	8.8	15.2	
Other beverages and tobacco†	5.6	6.0	6.0	
Watches†	6.6	12.1	19.4	
Subtotal (1)	*228.6*	*306.4*	*457.2*	*660.6*
Computers and office machines	33.4	41.3	65.0	89.0
Subtotal (2)	*262.0*	*347.7*	*522.2*	*749.6*
Cars	41.7	118.1	202.5	427.6
20% of other consumption goods	31.1	43.0	70.6	101.9
33% of parts (spare and assembly)	26.1	35.5	39.8	43.0
10% of capital and intermediate goods[a]	196.4	283.2	355.1	419.7
Subtotal (3)	*557.3*	*827.5*	*1,190.2*	*1,741.8*
50% of special transactions†	37.0	172.5	286.8	286.8[b]
Total	*594.3*	*1,000.0*	*1,477.0*	*2,028.6*

[a] Once all items already included separately are deducted.
[b] Estimated to equal the 1980 figure.

Source: Central Bank of Chile; except those marked with †: UN *International Trade Yearbook*, 1981.

Table 3.6
India: Imports of selected goods ($ million)

Item	1978	1979	1980	1981	(1978)	(1979)	(1980)	(1981)
Foodstuffs and live animals	287	297	410	541				
Raw materials (excl. fuels)	639	645	570	807				
Mineral fuels	1,973	3,023	6,167	6,308				
Animals and vegetable fats and oils	721	492	821	685				
Chemical products	885	1,062	1,416	1,352				
Basic manufactures	1,513	1,919	2,404	2,687				
Machinery and transport equipment of which:	1,399	1,463	1,803	1,823				
Agricultural machinery					17	12	20	53
Office machines					12	28	26	37
Vehicles					54	78	77	59
Parts for vehicles					49	62	55	52
Manufactures, miscellaneous	128	178	223	248				
Special transactions	14	33	2	3				
Totals	7,561	9,114	13,816	14,454				

Source: UN, *International Trade Yearbook* 1981, 1983.

Table 3.7
Superfluous imports in three developing countries, 1978–1981 ($ million)

Item	Mexico	Brazil	India
(i) *100% superfluous:*			
Beverages and tobacco	200	—	—
Office machines	692	760	103
TVs	506	—	—
Clothing	624	—	—
Photographic and film materials and equipment	187	524	—
Watches	205	189	—
Musical instruments and equipment	252	225	—
(ii) *50% superfluous:*			
Special transactions	5,388	—	26
(iii) *33% superfluous:*			
Vehicle parts	1,706	220	72
(iv) *20% superfluous:*			
Other miscellaneous manufactures	409	246	155
(v) *10% superfluous:*			
Raw materials, fuels, chemical products, basic manufactures, machinery and transport equipment	4,123	7,369	3,656
Total	*14,292*	*9,533*	*4,012*

Source: Based on Tables 3.1, 3.2, 3.6

Table 3.8
Comparison of some economic indicators, India and three Latin American countries, 1981

Country	Population (million)	GNP		External Debt		Superfluous imports 1978–81	
		Total ($ bn)	Per Capita ($)[a]	Total ($ bn)	Per Capita ($)	Total ($ bn)[d]	Per Capita ($)
Brazil	120.5	267.5	2,220	92[b]	763	9.5	79
Chile	11.3	28.9	2,560	18[b]	1,593	5.1	451
México	71.2	160.2	2,250	89[b]	1,250	14.3	200
India	690.1	179.4	260	20[c]	29	4.0	6

[a] Source, World Bank, *Annual Report*, 1983.
[b] Source, German Bank for South America, in *Excelsor* of Mexico, 20 June 1984.
[c] Estimate based on data from various sources, including World Bank.
[d] Based on tables 3.5 and 3.6.

Table 3.9
Developing countries: Distribution of military expenditure by major regions, and its share in GNP, 1970 and 1980
(at 1980 constant prices and rates of exchange)

Region	Total military expenditure ($ billion)		Military expenditure as percentage of GNP	
	1970	*1980*	*1970*	*1980*
West Asia	6.3	28.7	4.3	12.0
South Asia	3.4	5.1	2.9	3.1
East Asia	44.1	55.5	12.8	8.2
Africa	6.8	10.9	3.7	3.8
Latin America	4.8	7.0	1.4	1.2
Other developing countries	1.5	3.2	3.7	5.3
Total developing countries	*66.9*	*110.4*	*5.8*	*5.6*
Developed countries	349.7	383.6	6.2	4.6
World Total	*416.6*	*494.0**		

*This figure is very conservative; recent information on this subject indicates that present military expenditures are nearing $1,000 billion. But although the US substantially increased its defence expenditures under the Reagan Administration since early 1981, with the Soviet Union probably doing the same, it is highly doubtful that total military expenditure doubled in just five years.

Source: UN, *Disarmament,* vol VI, No. 3, Autumn/Winter 1983.

4   Waste and the Environment

Our second hypothesis is that the harmful effects of the prevailing development patterns in Latin American countries are not restricted to the economic and political spheres; there is also a very negative effect on the environment and on natural resources. We shall group these adverse effects on nature into two broad categories that are closely interlinked: firstly, pollution and toxic effects, and secondly the destruction of physical resources.

Pollution and toxic effects

We shall deal here with three major kinds of contamination: water pollution, air pollution and toxification linked to the use of chemical products, principally pesticides.

Water pollution, which, as is the case with all other forms of pollution, shows alarming rates of growth, is caused by a number of factors. The process of accelerated urbanization results in the proliferation of shanty-towns around the big Latin American cities, poorly equipped with sewage facilities (among other things). Because of the proximity of water wells to cesspools there is constant bacteriological contamination of the water, with extremely harmful effects on the health of those living in such marginal neighbourhoods. At the same time, the faecal waters of the big city, rife with infectious germs, merge with rivers and lakes which become, in the words of Wilheim, 'open sewers'.[49] Industrial discharges, mostly coming from big cities too, must also be counted. Food and beverage industries, textile, leather, pharmaceutical and other industries that produce finished goods mainly give rise to organic contamination. Their waste materials absorb oxygen from the water, thus damaging the normal development of aquatic flora and fauna. They also alter the ecological cycles in the affected and surrounding areas. Besides, the liquid residues of these types of industry are charged with solid elements in suspension that obstruct the normal flow of solar light to the bottom layers in rivers and lakes, thus jeopardizing the photosynthesis process required by deep aquatic flora as well as the normal ecological cycles. Those industrial plants producing intermediate goods, particularly petrochemicals, are prone to toxic contamination as a result of their residues of mercury, lead, cadmium, manganese, chromium, and radioactive materials. Cases of poisoning as a result of drinking contaminated water abound.[50]

The problem of toxic waste is, of course, much worse in industrial societies. According to recent information, there are over 80,000 toxic-material sites, with whole communities being poisoned by active chemical products, and their water reserves constantly affected by carcinogenic radiation. It was estimated that by end-1984 the total annual toxic disposal of US industries reached a level of 250 million tons of highly contaminating elements: that is, one metric ton per US inhabitant.[51] This is the model of society that dominant groups in Latin America and other Third World regions are trying to adopt at any cost.

The big city, as is well known by millions of stoic urbanites, also provokes a high degree of atmospheric pollution, causing severe health damage. Particularly serious are respiratory illnesses (such as emphysema, asthma, bronchitis, lung cancer), but there are also significant effects on cardiovascular, skin and eye problems. There are four major groups of atmospheric pollutants: various materials in suspension or particles, sulphur dioxide, carbon monoxide, and photochemical oxidants. The main polluting sources are industry and motor vehicles. In a large city like São Paulo, for example, the daily emission of pollutants is enormous: 500 tons of particle materials (70 per cent coming from industry), 900 tons of sulphur dioxide (90 per cent from fuel combustion), 5,000 tons of carbon monoxide (90 per cent from motor vehicles), and 1,200 tons of hydrocarbons and hydrogen dioxide (mostly from motor vehicles).[52] In Rio de Janeiro lead concentration in city tunnels and surrounding areas reach a level of four to five micrograms per cubic metre. One microgram only is the accepted norm. Measurements taken over a period of several years by the stations of the Pan-American Air Pollution Sampling Network show that 76 per cent of the collected samples of sedimental dust recorded very high pollution levels in relation to the UN World Health Organization (WHO) norms, 23 per cent in the case of particles in suspension, and 28 per cent in that of sulphur dioxide. Mexico City recorded the highest figures for sedimental dust: 2.11 to 3.26 mg per sq. cm., while the reference level is barely 0.5 mg per sq. cm. In the case of particles in suspension, a number of cities showed values that were higher than the reference level of 100 micrograms per cu.m.: São Paulo (169) Mexico City (145), Buenos Aires (167), and so forth. As to sulphur dioxide, the level of 70 micrograms per cu. m. was exceeded by Mexico City (147), Caracas (136), Santiago (81), and other cities.[53]

Production and utilization of energy also have a polluting effect on air, water and soil. In different ways, coal, petroleum, natural gas and nuclear power – to cite just the most damaging sources – cause considerable harm to the environment. It is estimated that pollution suffered by seas adjacent to Latin American and Caribbean shores is enormous, stemming from normal fuel discharges, reaching a level of some half a million tons a year, without considering major accidents (remember, for example, the severe ecological damage produced in the marine habitat by just two major incidents that took place in 1978/9: the sinking of the oil tanker Amoco-Cadiz, with around 1.8 million barrels of oil, and the accident at the oil well IXTOC 1, on the shores of Mexico, which resulted in a spill of nearly 3 million barrels. Trenova[54] indicates the following main effects that are or can be present in the various phases of primary production, refining, transport and final consumption of four fuels.

Coal: atmospheric contamination through combustion, burning of residues or fine coal particles, ashes, carbon, sulphur and nitrogen compounds; water pollution through mine drainage systems and washing processes.

Oil: air pollution through combustion, combustion gases of petroleum by-products and dust particles; water pollution through elimination of salt water residues, through accidents during drilling operations, and through thermal discharges and spillage during transportation;[55] contamination of the soil due to accidents suffered by oil pipe lines.

Natural gas: air pollution due to combustion of output surpluses and accidents suffered by gas pipes; water temperature alternations.

Nuclear energy: radioactive contamination, thermal water pollution, radioactive waste.

Toxic pollution by pesticides affects not only those people that have to apply them but also the population at large through contamination of food. Third World countries, subjected to massive publicity campaigns by transnational chemical corporations, become an important market for these lethal products, which are mainly produced in the North (total world output is estimated at over 2 million tons a year, i.e. half a kilo for each person on earth[56]). According to WHO data, the use of pesticides poisons one person every minute and kills one every $1\frac{3}{4}$ hours in the Third World. The US Natural Resources Defense Council estimates that in the developing world some 750,000 people are poisoned every year by pesticides. Most commonly-used pesticides attack the nervous system. Depending on the quantity, symptoms may range from a light indisposition to nausea, vomiting, convulsions, cardiac arrythmia and death. Sustained exposure to between low and moderate doses can produce, in the long term, cancer, infertility and genetic defects. Babies born in today's world are carriers of dangerous pesticides that they have absorbed in the maternal placenta; after birth, they continue being poisoned through the mother's milk, which is also contaminated. Studies carried out in Mexico, Colombia and other countries have detected high concentrations of DDT and other dangerous pesticides that are forbidden in the US and European countries; thus, the purest and safest of all nourishment is being transformed into a potentially dangerous food! But babies would not gain much if mother's milk were to be replaced by cow's milk, particularly in its processed forms (which would certainly please some transnational corporations) because cow's milk is even more contaminated, as several investigations and measurements have shown.

Research done in Colombia on organochlorate residues found in milk and other food products, has revealed the existence of very high levels of dangerous residues, well above those accepted as safe by the WHO. In the case of milk, for example, concentrations of Aldrin were found to be 15 times higher than the norm; those of Dieldrin were 26 times higher; in the case of Chlordane, 5 times higher; as to Endrin and Heptachlore, whose tolerance is zero, high concentrations were also found. All these pesticides are widely used by Latin American farmers.[57]

US legislation is very severe concerning the use of pesticides on US territory. Many dangerous products have been totally forbidden. However, producing companies continue exporting such products to Third World countries or, to avoid legal obstacles, simply transfer the plants themselves to the developing nations.* The paradox here is that the pollutants have begun to re-enter the US, contained in the food imported from the Third World. As a consequence, the US Government has imposed import restrictions on a number of fruit and vegetable products, affecting Mexico in a particularly hard way. The moral of this story is quite clear: the profits of pesticides can enter the US but not their noxious effects; these must be totally absorbed by the people living in the South!

Destruction of resources

Deterioration of Latin American ecosystems began with the Spanish conquest, when the intensive exploitation of mineral fields started. Areas that had been the site of prosperous agricultural activities in pre-Hispanic times soon began showing advanced soil erosion. While pre-Hispanic civilizations were culturally integrated with their natural habitat, since conservation of soil, water and forest resources meant their survival as human species, for the Spaniards these resources were considered as mere factors in the mining activity, which required large quantities of firewood. All forestry resources close to the mining areas were consumed. 'Mines were abandoned not because of their ore exhaustion, but because of problems linked to the availability of sufficient quantities of water for the

---

*For example, the Velsicol Chemical Corporation of Chicago, a company that has been involved in many environmental disasters, has a plant in Mexico that manufactures what it calls, with great ambiguity, 'chemical products for agriculture'. But Velsicol is famous for selling abroad a highly toxic product – lephtophos – under the commerical name of Fosvel, which attacks the human body like serpent's venom. Although this firm has declared that it does not continue manufacturing this toxic pesticide anywhere in the world, documents from the Costa Rican·government reveal that Velsicol is still selling Fosvel in the international market.[58]

concentration process, and to the exhaustion of firewood for melting'.[59] But mining was not the only source of soil deterioration; overgrazing caused similar problems. Other agricultural activities could be blamed as well. In tropical areas, by the end of the last century, crops such as coffee were causing severe ecological damage through itinerant cultivation and soil depletion. Halperin[60] indicates that 'the coffee area is a moving strip that leaves in its wake semi-devastated lands'. This sad story is repeated in different periods and geographical regions all over our planet. Present production and consumption schemes reproduce, on a much larger scale and at an accelerated pace, the depredatory actions of the Spanish and Portuguese conquerors, and of those who followed them.

According to estimates made by a number of scientists, every year the world loses twice the amount of agricultural land that is added. An area bigger than Britain is disappearing every year.[61] The UN Environment Programme has estimated that in the next 20 years some 600 million hectares of agricultural land will be lost due to erosion, urbanization and other forms of soil degradation, which is about half of all agricultural land under cultivation in 1975; even if some 300 million hectares of new agricultural land are likely to become productive, the net loss would still be 300 million hectares, or 25 per cent, which represents an alarming rate. Desertification is advancing everywhere, particularly in the Third World (recent information indicates that it is very difficult to distinguish the border between the Sahara and the Sahelian region in Africa), mainly as a result of deforestation, overgrazing and improper land management. During the first eight decades of the present century more than half of the forested area in developing nations has been destroyed. Indiscriminate tree felling for industrial purposes, for providing firewood or simply for clearing land required for cultivation, is leading the planet Earth to an ecological catastrophe. Only about one thousand million hectares of tropical forests are left, and they are being depleted at a rate of nearly two per cent a year. This means that unless some drastic corrective measures are adopted soon, those forests will disappear *completely,* in approximately fifty years from now.

Deforestation causes soil erosion, because the natural protection against rain is lost; the torrential rains in tropical areas wash the topsoil off into rivers, irrigation and drainage canals and to the sea. In turn, obstruction of drainage facilities causes progressive salinization of the soil. The wind, subsequently, completes the destructive pattern. Part of the forest destruction can be directly attributed to the profit-seeking motives of industrial companies. But it is also a consequence of the extreme poverty of many rural groups, who have constantly to cut the forest in order to supply themselves with the firewood they need to cook and to keep warm, and also to clear the land so that they can plant their subsistence crops. With the advance of commercial agriculture and ranching, large numbers of the impoverished rural population are gradually pushed toward the forest and mountainous areas, thus accelerating the process of forest destruction. The subsequent erosion and loss of agricultural soils force many of these people to migrate to the cities, thus accelerating the rate of urbanization and hence of forest and soil destruction.

According to Wilheim,[62] the State of São Paulo in Brazil today has only three per cent of its original forests, because of land fractioning, road construction and urbanization. The constant demand for land suitable for housing causes the urban area to expand at a frantic pace (Mexico City, for instance, grew more than ten times in area between 1910 and 1970). The poorer segments of the population are constantly pushed toward more distant and less accessible places, along with the revalorization of the more central sites they occupy. Those new plots do not normally have adequate services of any kind. The land there is continuously subdivided into ever smaller plots; in many cases such subdivision is carried out without official permission or knowledge, something that makes it even more difficult to have them properly serviced. Streets remain without pavements, sewage or drainage, with nothing that might remotely resemble some kind of paving. Thus, when it rains – and rains can be torrential in many of these cities – water opens deep furrows, destroys the hillsides, washes down the earth, obstructing any channel that may exist, causing extensive flooding and destroying the humble dwellings of the poor people living in those quarters. This vicious circle – a product of 'progress' – together with the rapid demographic growth recorded in most Latin American countries, are threatening to convert this region into a virtual desert in the not-too-distant future.

If the rate of extraction of world mineral resources continues as it has done over the past 40 or 50 years, due to the insatiable appetite of industrialized nations, proven reserves of some important minerals will most likely be exhausted before the mid-21st Century. To give an idea of what US mineral consumption patterns really mean, Preston Cloud, a well-known specialist, estimated in the early 1970s[63] what the result would be of increasing per capita world consumption levels to those prevailing in the US. For some of the most representative mineral resources the results were as follows: 30 billion tons of iron per year; 500 millions tons of lead, and 330 million tons of tin. These figures represent between 100 and 200 times the present annual output of the three minerals. Were such a scheme extrapolated to cover a world population of seven billion (as expected by the turn of the century) figures would have to double, on the assumption that US per capita consumption remains constant. In Cloud's view, it might be possible to satisfy the demand for iron, but not that of the other two metals, since their known reserves are too small.

Even if present world income and consumption schemes were to remain unaltered, such a high level of mineral utilization as that recorded by the US, Europe and Japan would anyway mean the depletion of known world reserves within relatively short time spans. A study carried out in 1975 by the US Bureau of Mines,[64] indicates that known world reserves in 1974 of sulphur, copper, gold, lead, molybdenum, tin, tungsten and zinc, among others, were only one and a half times the total world accumulated demand foreseen for the period 1974-2000. Silver would not cover even half of that demand, whereas in the case of a few other minerals it would be amply exceeded: in that of aluminium, reserves represented four times the foreseen accumulated demand until year 2000; those of iron 4.5 times; manganese 4.9 times; chromium 5.7 times. Cobalt, nickel and phosphates were in an intermediate position with reserves being two to three times higher than accumulated foreseen demand.

It is probable that the reserve situation has changed since 1974, due to the finding of new mineral fields, particularly in the sea bed.* At the same time, the fact that prices of silver, gold, copper and other metals have remained low or declined even further during recent years† indicates that metal markets are not yet showing any trace of anguish over a possible depletion of resources in the short term. Nevertheless, even if the reserves/ consumption (1974-2000) ratio were in fact double that estimated by the US Bureau of Mines, those minerals would arrive at their exhaustion point only a few decades later. Thus, in the case of copper, zinc, tungsten and tin, depletion would take place around the years 2030-2040. Even in the case of iron and aluminium, which are more abundant, known reserves may last for another century, or two centuries if reserves turn out to be double the proven magnitudes.

There are, of course, a number of factors that might influence those calculations in opposite ways. One of them is the variability of reserves to which we have referred above; another factor is the possible increase in metal prices when they come close to their depletion points. This would tend to depress consumption and favour their substitution by cheaper and more abundant materials; this, in turn, would prolong the reserve's useful life, pressing metal prices down and consumption up: a new cycle would thus be started, although the trend for average prices would be upwards. On the other hand, consumers might not come back to utilize a traditional specific metal once it has been substituted; this would again tend to increase the reserves' life expectancy.

But all this might be counterbalanced by a third factor: the persistence in

---

*Although the total stock of minerals contained in the earth's crust is fixed, known reserves vary with time, along with the discovery of new mineral fields amenable to exploitation. For example, known reserves of iron increased from 30 billion tons in 1946 to 110 billion tons in 1975, despite the enormous consumption recorded during those 30 years; those of copper went up from 100 to almost 400 million tons during the same period. Copper reserves in Chile and Peru, taken jointly, increased from 59 million tons in 1960 to 105 million tons in 1975.[65]

†Prices of copper, zinc, aluminium and other raw materials fell sharply during the second quarter of 1984, and have continued falling since then. According to the Swiss firm Haenkel-Foster, during the period March–June 1984, prices of zinc went down by 18 per cent, copper 16 per cent and aluminium 13 per cent.[66]

industrial nations of relatively high rates of economic growth, which would translate into ever increasing consumption of raw materials, even allowing for a certain degree of substitution.

We are not in a position to estimate the quantitative effects on the longevity of mineral resources of factors such as technological change and substitution processes. But we might gain a faint idea about the impact that GNP growth in industrial nations could have on future consumption of such resources. With this objective in view, we did the following arithmetic exercise. If per capita GNP in industrialized nations were to increase during the next 100 years at an annual rate of 1.5 per cent, and population at 0.5 per cent a year, this would mean that in year 2085 GNP per capita would reach an average figure of around $45,000 (at 1985 prices), which is roughly 4.5 times the current average. Total GNP would then be seven times higher. Unless very drastic changes in the composition of demand take place – for instance, that practically all of the increase in GNP were to correspond to additional output of services and not to material goods, or that substantial improvements occur in the metal utilization rate per unit of finished goods, or that massive substitution is effected – it is quite likely that mineral consumption by industrial nations will tend to be much higher than that predicted by the US Bureau of Mines. In that case, exhaustion of reserves would occur sooner than estimated above.

The central argument of the optimists and anti-catastrophists, who, quite naively, believe that minerals will last almost forever, no matter what the rates of extraction are, rests on two basic assumptions: firstly that such materials are extremely abundant in the earth's crust (including the vast marine deposits), and secondly that, once they are processed and manufactured, metals can be used again through recycling.

Regarding the first point, the argument is refuted by Tilton (see reference 65) who has made some very interesting calculations on the 'life expectancy' of certain minerals according to different rates of consumption growth. As a starting reference point he takes the total stock of minerals contained in the earth's crust, which is many million times higher than the reserves so far identified. This eliminates the problem of having to work on the basis of 'reserves' – as we have seen, an extremely flexible concept. His framework is the *maximum limit* of resources that exist in the earth's crust. According to such calculations, if production were to remain constant at present levels, the crust could provide copper for another 200 million years, lead for 84 million years, iron for 2.6 billion years and zinc for 400 billion years. That is, if no technological or other restrictions on the utilization of those minerals are taken into account, the planet could supply an adequate amount of metals practically forever. But this panorama changes radically when a growth coefficient is introduced, even if this is small. Thus, with a rate of production growth of 2 per cent, copper resources are exhausted after 770 years and those of iron after 900 years, to mention just two cases. If the rate of extraction growth goes up to 5 per cent (which is close to that recorded historically between 1947 and 1974 for several minerals) the exhaustion periods are reduced to less than half: 330 years in the case of copper, 380 years in that of iron, and similarly for other minerals. These calculations do not admit any juggling and show quite dramatically what the real limits are to a continued increase in the use of non-renewable resources. As to our second point, even considering the possibilities of recycling – which have their own limits in the availability of energy – the real ceiling for the use of metals may be lower than that signalled by the preceding figures, since it is highly improbable that the entire mineral stock, to the last kilogram, can be extracted from the earth's crust. To the enormous physical and economic difficulties involved in such an operation, one must add the gigantic increase in waste and pollution caused by the exploitation of fields that are progressively poorer, by the destruction of massive amounts of soil to extract less and less mineral per ton of earth removed, and by the growing amounts of energy needed.

On the other hand, a continuous increase in mineral consumption by the North will inevitably mean the spoliation of resources that are mainly concentrated in the territories of Third World countries. We have already seen how, through such mechanisms as foreign indebtedness, growth in interest rates, and foreign trade expansion, this plunder is already taking place, albeit in a rather gradual and apparently peaceful way. At present there is a high degree of dependence of Northern countries on supplies from the South of a large number of strategic materials. The US, for instance, depends wholly or almost wholly on Third World countries to obtain strontium, tin, columbium, graphite, chromium, manganese, bauxite, and, to a lesser extent, platinum, tungsten, antimony, cobalt and others. Despoliation is inevitable, unless consumption and production patterns change dramatically both in the North and in the South.

Water is another basic resource that is being excessively consumed and depleted. This is the most essential resource for life sustenance. We can stop consuming other goods and may remain without any solid food for a good number of days, but we cannot survive without water for more than a few days. Nevertheless, and despite the fact that water is also a limited resource, societies are wasting it in a truly scandalous way. The biological minimum required by an individual to survive is around one quarter of a gallon or little less than one litre per day. But, besides this vital minimum, large quantities of water are required for cooking, washing, producing food and, in general, for the carrying out of practically all productive processes. For instance, the output of one kilogram of beef ready for consumption requires several thousand litres of water; nearly half a million litres are needed to carry out all extractive and industrial processes associated with the manufacture of one car.[67]

Although two-thirds of the Earth's surface consists of water, barely 3 per cent of it is fresh water, and of that only a minimal portion is drinking water. Besides, this resource is unequally distributed among different regions; this factor, added to differences in wealth and development, results in huge variations in availability and consumption per person. In a semi-arid region of the US, such as the State of Arizona, the daily water consumption per person is estimated by Barnet[68] at about 600 litres (150 gallons); in a semi-arid zone of Africa such consumption barely reaches 3 litres, (eight-tenths of a gallon). But these figures correspond to direct consumption only; if other requirements are added, in the US of today average per capita consumption of water reaches the astounding figure of 6,000 litres a day. Although an important proportion of the water used in industries and homes is recycled, about one quarter of the total is lost through pollution and inadequate management.

In many Third World countries there is great scarcity of water, not only for domestic use but also for agricultural and industrial purposes. There are large segments of the population that do not have easy access even to minimal quantities of drinking water. This leads to very high disease and death rates, particularly among children, who are victims of diarrhoea and a number of infectious and parasitic diseases caused by the ingestion of contaminated water. Nevertheless, even under these conditions, considerable wastage of water is recorded by those who have the luck or the money to enjoy an easier access to this resource. It is easy to observe in big cities how enormous quantities of drinking water are used in garden irrigation, in car washing, in filling pools, or in those endless baths that are taken by many wealthy people. As water is practically cost-free almost everywhere, there are no restrictions to limit its wastage. If water were appraised at its real value – that is, considering its finite nature and the financial replacement costs of present sources – and priced accordingly, with progressively higher tariffs, its patterns of consumption would most likely be quite different.

5   In Search of a New Path

We do not wish, in this chapter, to judge the merits of the individual renegotiation agreements that many Latin American countries have so far reached with creditor governments or institutions, nor the advantages/disadvantages of the more or less collective strategies that are being pursued by Latin America and the Third World in general, in relation to the debt problem (which constitute, to a large extent, a prolongation of the efforts that Third World countries have been making for years towards the establishment of a New International Economic Order). We believe that most of what has been done or proposed in this field has been restricted to what one could call the purely technical or book-keeping aspects. So far, the profound socio-political problems that mar these countries' external relations have not been tackled. Further loans, concession of additional time to repay the debt, granting a few years' grace, and so forth, are measures that will probably alleviate the pressure on the debtors' economies, but they will not help in modifying the latter's present dependency ties with the North. Resource-flow from South to North will continue unabated, as will wasteful and depredatory consumption-production-development practices.

It is for this reason that we shall not enter into a detailed discussion of what was said in Quito, Cartagena, Buenos Aires or Montevideo, at the meetings held by the Cartagena Group; nor shall we examine what was debated at the annual conferences of the IMF/World Bank, the United Nations Conference on Trade and Development (UNCTAD) or the Economic Commission for Latin America. What we will attempt to do here is to explore instead some possible avenues that may eventually lead to the elimination of the triple exploitation we have referred to in various passages of this book: that suffered by Latin American and other Third World nations, that experienced by the majority of the population within Third World countries, and finally that suffered by nature on account of human abuse.

We wish to promote the search for paths that may help societies to become rationally ordered, where individuals and social groups may live in harmony with each other and with the ecosystem, while preserving that ecosystem as a support suitable for future generations.

To aid this exploratory task we have divided this chapter into four sections: the limits to consumption; propaganda and the myth of progress; a reasonable option to resolve the present debt problem; and going beyond dependency, through elimination of the basic causes of indebtedness and social waste.

The limits to consumption

Both from a Third World and a planetary viewpoint, an indefinite continuation of 'American-style' consumption patterns becomes unbearable. Equally intolerable is the unlimited growth in population. But, look out! The entire burden of the responsibility for resource depletion and destruction is usually laid upon demographic growth in Southern countries. However, if the problem is examined from the perspective of their share in global resource utilization or consumption, it will be found that the major responsibility falls on the shoulders of North-Western countries and not on those of the South. The reason is very simple: each north-westerner consumes on average about 15 times more resources than a typical inhabitant of a poor country in the Third World. (It is estimated that an average US citizen consumes around 300 times the energy used by the average African.) Even if differences in population growth rates between South and North were 3 or 4 to 1, (which is hardly the case), it would be more 'convenient' for humankind as a whole that the north-westerners stopped reproducing before the southerners did the same, since one unborn north-westerner would save more resources than four, five or even ten southerners that remain unborn. (The concept of north-westerners also includes the southern elites, since they are excessive consumers as well.)

Obviously, the above does not mean that population in the South can continue growing as it has done in the past simply because the majority of it consumes very little. Should the imbalances in the present economic-political structures and relations be corrected – both within countries and between countries – those population groups would have to consume more, as a minimum until they satisfy their essential needs. There are many who argue that this is the *only* effective formula to control demographic growth. We do not think so. We believe that there is no incompatibility between vigorous demographic policies and an equally forceful socio-economic and political reorientation. From the point of view of resource utilization it is not the same thing to satisfy the essential needs of 8,000 as of 30,000 million people. Their numbers will be limited, therefore, by the availability of resources. Conversely, the extent to which those needs may be satisfied will be determined – once distribution problems have been overcome – by the number of individuals whose needs have to be met, and by the height at which the ceiling of those needs is placed. The greater the number of people and the size of their respective demands (the 'ceiling'), the fewer will be the possibilities to satisfy them all, and the smaller will be the number of future generations on earth that will have access to finite resources.

Responding to this awareness, various schools of thought have proposed 'zero growth' in industrialized nations, considering that they have not only reached, but certainly exceeded, the point of entirely satisfying the essential needs of the population, with only some distribution problems remaining to be solved. There are others, however, that state that these arguments in favour of zero economic growth in the US are based on false premises. Lester Thurow, for instance, tries to demonstrate that arguments such as the one we presented earlier when citing Cloud, are invalid. Thurow says:

> In the context of zero economic growth . . . a fallacious 'impossibility' argument is often made to demonstrate the need for zero economic growth. The argument starts with a question: How many tons of this or that non-renewable natural resource would the world need if everyone in the world now had the consumption standards enjoyed by those in the US? The answer is designed to be a mind-boggling number in comparison with current supplies of such resources. The problem with both the question and the answer is that it assumes that the rest of the world is going to achieve the consumption standards of the average American without at the same time achieving the productivity standards of the average American. This is, of course, algebraically impossible. The world can only consume what it can produce. When the rest of the world has consumption standards equal to those of the US, it will be producing at the same rate and providing as much of an increment to the world-wide supplies of goods and services as it does to the demands for goods and services.[69]

This is a most remarkable counter-argument, of a wonderful arithmetical simplicity! What it shows is that Thurow, as well as other economists and scientists that are opposed to the zero economic growth notion, do not understand the real sense of the argument, nor do they understand where the heart of the problem lies. It is obvious that the world cannot consume what has not been produced. But what exercises such as Cloud's try to demonstrate is not that per capita consumption of Third World peoples should increase to match the US, Swiss or Danish standards, but that the latter should come down to stay at a reasonable level. We have already seen that were the north-westerners to continue augmenting their consumption at present rates, many natural resources would be depleted in the not too distant future; by then, even the American or European citizens belonging to those future generations will have to renounce consumption of what is not available within the limits of our planet in an accessible way.

There are other scientists who, even with quite a different orientation from Thurow's, are equally doubtful that availability of physical resources constitutes a limiting factor for the achievement of an adequate welfare level for humankind as a whole. The Bariloche Group, for instance, formulated by the mid-1970s a detailed world development model[70] whose fundamental target was the attainment of a higher degree of equity between and within nations, as well as the full satisfaction of all the world population's basic needs. The model assumed that mineral reserves suffice to keep the planet's population over millions of years. Besides, it excluded pollution as a possible obstacle for the achievement of an economic growth rate that permits every human being on earth to reach an adequate livelihood. It is argued, in this respect, that adequate control measures (the cost of which would be only a tiny fraction of the world's total GNP) would eliminate a sizeable part of the problem. The conclusion, therefore, is that economic growth is not necessarily linked to an increase in pollution. On the other hand, the model attempts to describe the behaviour of a society that, in principle, lives in harmony with its environment. Such compatibility would fundamentally depend on the existence of an economic system that limits its output to those basic and cultural goods that humankind really needs, thus avoiding the overutilization of resources; once basic needs have been satisfied, the rate of economic growth would decline so that, even if the range of social options continues to increase, environmental damage may be kept at low levels. Such a decrease in economic activity would imply an increase in free time, which in itself represents an increment in the number of cultural options which, however, would create minimum demands on the productive sectors. So far so good! We cannot but agree with all this. There seems to be no disagreement with what we have been proposing throughout this book. But in fact this is not so. The Bariloche model has a serious internal contradiction, that leads it to a final position which is 180 degrees opposed to ours and even to their own stated principles. In fact, the model not only does not postulate zero, or close to zero economic growth, as might have been interpreted, at least for that phase that extends from having achieved full satisfaction of basic needs, but in its mathematical formulations it conceives a growth that is *enormous* for both developed and developing nations.

The model foresees a per capita GNP growth in developed countries of nearly seven times during the hundred years between 1960 and 2060 (i.e. higher than our own assumption in the exercise above), notwithstanding the fact that even at the starting point most of the essential needs of the population in these countries had already been met, and for a good part of it they had been amply exceeded. Hence, almost all of the increment should be regarded as excess product or waste – five or six times the total per capita product in 1960. Unless a large portion of the increment in GNP derives from purely cultural activities, a possibility which seems quite unreal, it is hard, not to say impossible, to be unaware that such excessive economic growth in the North will inevitably lead to massive despoliation and de-struction of Third World mineral and other resources. For developing nations the Bariloche Group also foresees a GNP expansion that goes well beyond the point when all basic needs are fully met. In the case of Latin America, this point would be attained by the end of the 20th century, when per capita GNP reaches an average level of $809 (1960 prices); the projection, however, pushes the per capita GNP in the year 2060 to over $5,700 (1960 prices), which is seven times that required to satisfy the basic needs of all the population. Something similar is projected for Asia and Africa, although with slightly less ambitious targets.

Is this vision a cornucopian one, prompted by the notion that resources do not limit economic expansion? Or do they intend to achieve just a minuscule narrowing of the relative gap between rich and poor, even if in absolute terms the gap will continue increasing? Isn't there a fundamental contradiction between the various postulates of the model? We present this contradictory Bariloche Group position because there are other schools of progressive thought in Latin America and other parts of the world that stick to these kinds of postulates. It is difficult to understand how projections of this type, which imply the generation of an enormous excess product, match the stated objectives for the new society. This particularly concerns the attainment of more equitable relationships at the international and domestic levels, or the establishment of non-consumerist values, both of which presuppose production for social needs and not for profit.

The idea of 'growth at any cost' is imbedded in the prevailing schools of thought in Third World countries. Their demands for a New International Economic Order are centred around the wish to have a larger share of the world's economic pie, on the understanding that the pie will continue growing indefinitely. As we have seen, this goes hand in hand with swelling imports, with increasing indebtedness and with asphyxiating dependency.* No authorized voices have been heard to say: for some people to go up the socio-economic ladder others will have to come down! This – which should hold not only among countries but especially within countries – is simply not proposed. On the contrary, poorer nations trust that the richer ones may continue expanding their economies at ever-increasing rates, so that the latter may buy more goods from them – even if they are for lethal or wasteful purposes – and thus remain in a position to keep their own development schemes unaltered, schemes that are just as inequitable and destructive. The high price paid for such a privilege is even tighter dependency and the loss of the material base needed to sustain future generations.

Evidently, such a state of affairs cannot continue for much longer. The

---

*In a recent document, *The Crisis in Latin America: Evolution and Perspectives* (E/CEPAL/G.1294, of 9 February 1984) the Economic Commission for Latin America states that the very large increase in Latin American imports 'was vital for the maintenance of economic growth and liberalization policies, as well as anti-inflationary policies'. From what we have discussed so far it seems evident that such an increment was basically intended to keep up or exacerbate irrational and wasteful consumption patterns.

tempo of the production-destruction process has accelerated too much, to the point where it is seriously threatening the future of humankind. The gap between the rich and the poor widens, and with it the repression against the latter becomes stronger. Entropy, a central concept of the second law of thermodynamics, increases; that is, there is less and less energy available to be transformed into work. Each time that energy is extracted from the environment to be transformed through the social mechanisms and processes, a part of it is dissipated and wasted, until all of it, including that which has been transformed into goods, ends in one way or another as waste.[71] All metabolic and technological processes are irreversibly entropic processes.[72] Pollution is just the total sum of available energy that has been converted into unavailable energy. Waste is dissipated energy; pollution is, therefore, another name for entropy.[73] Each time that, somewhere, local entropy is diminished, through the action of machines or human beings, there is a correspondingly larger increase in entropy in neighbouring places; thus, the net change in total entropy has always a positive sign; this is, of course, a negative fact for humankind.

Having reached this point, we have to face the crucial question about *who decides what is essential and what is superfluous.* Will it be the state, through its dominant bureaucrats? Will some social planners be in charge of this task? Will the base communities themselves decide? Is it indispensable that somebody *has to decide?* In market economies these questions have been answered by the market itself: it is the market that decides what to produce, what to consume, how much each person will receive, and what price will have to be paid for that 'much'. But we have seen that the market is irrational and unjust, since some people consume too much while others lack the most essential things. Market defenders will most likely insist that it is preferable to suffer the inequalities and irrationalities of the system (although they will probably deny the charges) rather than suffer the totalitarianism of externally imposed decisions. For market defenders what is really at stake is the 'freedom to choose', postulated so forcefully by Milton Friedman. They will even maintain that what is irrational for us is perfectly rational for them; they will also state that those goods we deem to be superfluous may be essential for others: if not, why would they consume them in ever growing quantities? Moreover, there are many who would like to consume such goods but are not in a position to do so. Why then forbid them? Besides, why should we care *now* about what may happen in the year 2500 when people will know what to do with their lives and how to solve their problems *at that time?*

To these and many other questions or counter-arguments we can only answer that we are simply exposing some very concrete and absurd facts, such as the gigantic inequities in wealth and income distribution, the rapid pace of natural resources destruction, the irrational waste of all kinds of goods by a few, the growing loss of economic and political sovereignty of Third World countries, the systematic despoliation they are suffering, and so forth. We will be told, most likely, that such phenomena constitute the temporary price that has to be paid for the attainment and upkeep of 'freedom'. But such a price of freedom sounds very much like the argument in favour of foreign indebtedness: it is just a temporary expedient. However, we also know that in reality the opposite has been true: not only has debt not been temporary, but it has persisted with increasing force and perversity. The same thing is applicable to social irrationality and inequity: they tend to become deeper with the passage of time, and to become more malignant. Elsewhere[74] we have reflected about the true meaning of the concept 'freedom to choose', which is valid for only a small number of privileged people. For the impoverished majority, market dictatorship is the worst and most permanent form of oppression, and for humankind as a whole the surest and quickest way to collective suicide.

On the other hand, if we go back to the origins of the capitalist system we can realize that what the system promised, its morality – frugality, puritanism, abstinence, the capitalists sacrifice in not consuming more than the bare minimum, providing a just remuneration to each one according to his/her participation in the process of national wealth creation – has not been accomplished at all. Market hedonism has degenerated even the system's own principles. Therefore, the libertarian arguments that might oppose our assessments and reflections are but mere manifestations of those who want to keep their privileges intact, or even increase them, to the detriment of the true freedom of the majorities, which can be summarized as the possibility of autonomously exercising their rights as human beings.

At the same time, we can state at this stage that, unless very profound political, social and economic changes are undertaken, the earth will become a battleground in which, not only will the dominant group be exerting the utmost brutality against the dominated one to extract the maximum possible surplus, but it will also be exerting the same brutality against the planet Earth itself. It is no wonder, therefore, that some scientists and futurologists are beginning to talk about the day when the humans will start colonizing space so that the planet Earth, once despoiled of its basic resources, can be abandoned. But we must be aware that, if such a moment arrives one day, only the first-class passengers will leave the spaceship earth; the others, the destitute, the 'wretched of the earth', as Fanon called them, will remain aboard, left behind to subsist or die with whatever is left, until the species is erased from the surface of this planet. Thus, the gap will eventually acquire a spatial dimension.

Propaganda and the myth of progress

Although we are not in a position to indicate who could assume the responsibility for judging or deciding what is essential or not in a rationally ordered society, we can certainly examine some of the modern propaganda techniques that are utilized by those who now decide; by those who are the judges and dictators of our behaviour.

So far, we have analysed the behaviour of modern society as a whole, without referring to individuals. We will now examine myths and what people conform to, their behavioural patterns in relation to other human beings, and to their natural and social environment.

Individuals' profound beliefs and their behaviour have religious and cultural roots. The majority of primitive religions saw nature as something sacred and, therefore, controlled human conduct in order to protect nature's delicate balance. By contrast, according to Culberson's analysis,[75] the Judeo-Christian culture, in placing man above nature, divorced him from his natural environment and allowed him to use it at his will, ignoring all of nature's laws. For this author, the theory of economic development is not based on scientific or ecological criteria. In fact, it derives from the Judeo-Christian cultural myth, according to which the universe gyrates around man, and it is assumed that with time it will ascend to a sublime position. In its secular version, this theory is the doctrine of progress.

In conformity with the doctrine of progress, Ellul says,[76] all nations that found their development on modern technology – capitalist and socialist alike – believe that continuous technological advance is the key for humankind to achieve and sustain a better quality of life. This doctrine, supported by the overwhelming capacity of propaganda to convince, has turned the myths of progress and modernization into a religious belief.

Modern technology and propaganda – the first increasingly destroying the environment and the second imposing myths and distorting the perception of reality – have created a new ecology. We live in it believing blindly in its advantages while remaining unconscious of its devastating effects.

The incredible effectiveness of modern propaganda – the techniques of which have developed more rapidly than the thinking capacity of the average human being – is due to the fact that it is based on the scientific analysis of psychology and sociology. The expert elaborates his propaganda strategies supported by his knowledge of society as well as of the individual's behavioural patterns, needs and conditioning.

The individuals who form mass society are constantly being conditioned and impelled to serve propaganda's hidden interests. Which are the mechanisms that propaganda utilizes to attain such objectives, and to what extent are people being dangerously manipulated? Ellul remarks in this respect that the human being is extremely malleable, lacking in self-confidence, capable of accepting and following advice from many different quarters, and is easily moved by all doctrinal currents.

The strategy of the modern propagandists, according to Ellul's analysis, is directed simultaneously to the individual and to the mass. These two elements cannot be dissociated, because the individual is affected by propaganda both as a member and a participant of such a mass.* The

*Mass society – a phenomenon of our times – is composed of lonely persons who have become
Continued

propagandist never visualizes humans as isolated beings, but in relation to what they have in common with each other: motivations, needs, feelings, and myths. Individuals who are immersed in the mass are subjected to the characteristic pressures that any person who forms part of a group experiences. They become more vulnerable to emotions such as sentimentalism, impulsiveness and immoderation; these reactions become stronger and then take hold of the whole group.

For propaganda's sake a person is never alone, but is always part of a group: the TV viewer, even if sitting alone, is part of a large group, and he/she is aware of this. Newspaper readers or radio listeners constitute a mass with an organic existence, even if scattered rather than gathered in a precise place. These individuals have access to the same sources of information, they receive the same publicity messages, be they of a commercial or a political nature. They see the same TV serials and admire the same heroes. Generally, they are affected by the same stimula, thus inducing similar reactions and ideas; they participate in the same myths. It is a psychological mass that, without knowing it, is constantly affected and influenced by the messages that the media are disseminating.

Each medium is appropriate for a given type of propaganda. Thus, to achieve maximum effectiveness, they must be complementary and all of them, without exception, have to be used, since not every one of them reaches the same public, nor in the same way. Propaganda must therefore be directed in accordance with its particular audience, trying at the same time to reach the widest possible number of persons. Without mass media there can be no modern propaganda. But for mass media to become a real instrument of manipulation they must be subjected to a central control with very well-defined objectives. The effects of the media will be even greater if they are concentrated in one single hand.

Propaganda seeks to surround the individual in all possible ways, acting upon the will, the feelings, and needs, through the conscious and the subconscious. The myth created by propaganda imposes upon individuals a complete set of truths that penetrate their spirit without the need for reasoning. The myth provides them with a coherent and comprehensible

Continued from page 101

disconnected, for different reasons, from the various organic groups that form society. Thus, they have lost the orientation which guided their lives. In Latin America, as in the rest of the Third World, because of extreme rural poverty millions of peasants migrate to the urban centres. Inhabitants of small towns abandon their place of origin to establish themselves in the capital or in other large cities, in search of better working opportunities. There are also those rebels who, because of their non-conformism or eagerness for freedom, break with their family ties, old friendship bonds and their home. All these individuals, physically and psychologically uprooted, can live together only in an unstructured society; that is, the mass society. All those who can once again incorporate themselves into organized groups such as political parties or labour organizations, stop belonging to the mass society. The others remain as isolated beings, much more unstable, without an orienting guide, and are easily trapped by propaganda.

explanation of the world that does not allow any discrepancy. Myths have such a powerful force that, once they are accepted, they control the whole of the individual; they make a person immune to any other influence and push him/her towards action, this being the ultimate purpose of propaganda.

Propaganda takes care of education because there cannot be a contradiction between education and propaganda. In order that the latter may penetrate, individuals must have a minimum of learning. Literacy is essential to initiate a person into consumerism or into a given ideology.

The most powerful manipulative system in any society is its network of schools. Even in the poorest countries, where only a small fraction of the population has access to education, that fraction provides the political, economic and social leaders for all the communities of the nation; what is taught to that élite, is, therefore, decisive. Each teacher in each school, from primary to higher education, is a propagandist by virtue of what he or she is, thinks or does. The education of the young is oriented in such a way as to condition them for what will follow. Schools and teaching methods are designed to integrate the child into the group of conformists. The essential role of propaganda through education is that of spreading social controls. The objective pursued is the achievement of consensus, so that the basic structures of present cultural and social institutions, especially those related to technological lifestyles in a free market economy, can be maintained, or so that doctrines favouring structural changes in a society undergoing revolutionary transformations can be taught.[77]

Modern propaganda must fill every moment in an individual's life: posters and loudspeakers outside; newspapers, radio and TV at home; meetings and cinema in the evening. It must create a complete environment for individuals, an environment from which they can never escape. To avoid points of reference and keep them isolated from everything coming from outside, censorship is applied. The purpose of modern propaganda is not that of changing affiliation to a doctrine or modifying an opinion, but rather to obtain the individual's irrational adherence to a myth that will push him/her towards a process of activity.[78]

Manipulation takes place in two different but combined stages: pre-propaganda and active propaganda. Without being aware, the individual is subjected for a long time to the influence of pre-propaganda, directed to create his/her conditioned reflexes and myths. These are achieved through a long and repetitive training, with certain signs or symbols, persons or facts, arousing inevitable reactions. Propaganda attempts to create myths with which people will live (for example technology, modernization, nationalism, and productivity). The myth pushes indivi-duals into action because it symbolizes everything that is good and desirable, just and truthful. As such, the myth has the power to take complete possession of the individual's mind. When conditioned reflexes have been created, and people live inside a collective myth, the moment has come when active propaganda can easily mobilize them for action. The visible and spectacular results of active propaganda are only possible thanks to the slow preparation of pre-propaganda.

Why is it that in contemporary society, people are obsessed by a notion of progress that is based on a continuous development of technology? To reach material objectives that symbolize a better quality of life is a strong aspiration that has spread together with the massive production of consumer goods and the world expansion of propaganda. That is why it is justifiable to think that, no matter how different are the explicit forms propaganda takes in different countries, it is always the same powerful interests that are acting behind it.

That is why it is not an easy task to counteract those values, beliefs and myths that are deeply imbedded in modern societies. It is a moral imperative, however, that leaders who are conscious of the malignant trends driving humankind to a true holocaust combine forces to exert political pressure against the establishment that benefits from the maintenance of the status quo. Some examples show that this is possible. The case of the various movements of ecologists, pacifists, anti-nuclear campaigners and others in the Federal Republic of Germany which united in 1980 to form Die Grünen (The Green Party), is the most successful one. They have achieved significant political power and are exercising considerable influence on decisions taken at state and federal levels. In the US, a number of ecologist groups, led by the National Wildlife Federation, after a prolonged period of intense campaigning and lobbying, were able to obtain in 1986 the passing of a law by the US Congress that makes it compulsory for multilateral credit institutions in which the US is represented to consider the ecological impact of any new development project to be financially assisted by those institutions.

The above are but a few hints of possible lines of action that might be followed to disarticulate the establishment forces and modify current trends, in pursuance of a rationally ordered society.

Payment of the debt

As indicated above, it was only in 1983–84, when the Latin American economic and financial crisis acquired ferocious strength, that governments in this region began an earnest search for a way out of the problem. Although the several meetings held so far by the Cartagena Group have meant some advance in exchange of information, or in coordination towards a joint position, no real progress has been made concerning the much-needed effort to achieve collective political negotiations. The US Government, band-leader of creditor governments and institutions, adamantly opposes any attempt by debtor nations to organize something that might remotely resemble a debtor's club. Their strength lies in a country-by-country approach, whereas this is precisely the main weakness in the position of debtor nations. For this reason, the mechanism that has so far been most used is that of rolling over the debts; payments of the principal that were to be made in 1983, 1984 and 1985 have been successively postponed into the future. In a few cases, the grace period has been quite long, but interest payments have to be paid punctually. The notable exceptions have been Bolivia and Peru. In all cases, however, the debt has continued growing, albeit more slowly.

The reason for such timid official Latin American behaviour lies perhaps in government fear of sharply breaking commercial and financial relations with the capitalist centres, and of having to stand the possible retaliatory measures of industrialized nations (for example, embargo of all merchandise arriving at US, European or other ports abroad, sequestration of air or maritime vessels, or cutting short-term export-import credit). Memories of how the US copper companies persecuted the Chilean red metal and other Chilean interests throughout the world, when the government and Congress of Chile approved the nationalization of copper mines in 1971, are still very vivid. It is doubtful, however, that such actions could be taken against the Latin American nations as a whole.

But there are additional reasons for Latin American reluctance to take more radical steps. Governments in this region do not really wish to create a situation whereby the international financial system might collapse. A simultaneous decision to default on the part of major Latin American debtors would undoubtedly provoke the bankruptcy of the largest US banks, and probably some European banks as well, no matter how much the banks' exposure and reserve-against-losses coefficient may have improved during the past couple of years. Even if European governments or those of the US and Japan were ready to bail out the affected banks (something that is not at all evident) and take over the responsibility of covering a large portion of the unpaid Latin American debt, just the knowledge of the accomplished default by Latin American nations would certainly spread panic amongst depositors and investors all over the world. The problem, therefore, would not be confined to just $40 or $50 billion of the Latin American annual service, or even to the $400 billion of the total Latin American foreign debt; it would cover practically all the monetary mass that circulates through national and international financial channels. It might become the crash that has been described in popular economic fiction, but a much weightier version.

But governments are not prepared to act together even in a less radical way. In 1985 President Castro of Cuba proposed the total cancellation of 'unpayable and uncollectable' Third World debts and suggested that a fraction of military expenditures might be sufficient to meet that end. In July 1985 President García of Peru declared, when taking over the Administration, that not more than ten per cent of export earnings would be devoted to debt repayments (a decision that other Latin American Governments may soon follow). But no other authorized voices have been heard South of the Rio Bravo in favour of a drastic change in terms and conditions for debt negotiations.

Obviously, if all the concessions being thought out and sought by Third World countries were to be granted, the economies of the Third World would undoubtedly be relieved to some extent. With lower amounts of exchange earnings going to debt repayment, there would be room to increase imports and thus 'reactivate' the affected economies. Without engaging for the time being in a discussion of what such a reactivation would really mean, considering that it would tend to perpetuate an economic growth model that we believe to be irrational and inequitable, we wish to point out certain deficiencies in the current approaches, the most important of which, in our view, is the rather lukewarm attitude towards tying prices of raw materials to rates of interest.

To illustrate this issue, let us repeat the exercise presented earlier, taking now the case of Mexican oil as an example. Mexico has to pay an annual interest bill of about $10 billion. At $15 per barrel (roughly the average world price at end-November 1986; prices received by Mexico were on the average somewhat lower), that sum represents the extraction and remittance of nearly 670 million barrels, or close to 1.6 million barrels a day, which is a higher volume than total present oil exports of Mexico. By November 1985 the interest payment would have required only 400 million barrels. But if the interest rate paid by Mexico were of only six per cent instead of the present average of ten per cent, the volume of oil required to pay the annual interest bill would only be some 240 million barrels a year (at November 1985 prices). This clearly shows that Mexico is giving away over 400 million barrels of oil per year in exchange for nothing.

This crucial point, the terms of trade between the cost of international money and Latin American (and Third World, in general) export prices, is not being considered. The monstrosity of this forced tribute can be fully appreciated when seen in the light of the finite nature of the resources being remitted. The extra 430 million barrels of oil that Mexico is forced to give away every year represent about one per cent of its total oil reserves; if this brilliant operation continued for another 20 years, Mexico would have gratuitously relinquished one-fifth of its total petroleum resources. Considering that domestic consumption of oil in Mexico is around 450 million barrels per year, the 'donation' would represent about 18 or 19 years of security for domestic supplies.

Something similar can be said of Chilean and Peruvian copper, of Bolivian tin, and so forth. It is because of this fact that we believe that the destruction and despoliation of Latin American and other Third World resources is an intolerable and unacceptable process. However, nothing serious is being done in that respect. The various formulae that are being considered to deal with the debt problem are totally insufficient and also deficient. On the side of the debtors, the Group of Cartagena declarations are still far away from tackling the central issues so far described, which require, anyway, a collective approach. On the lenders' side, a special mention should be made of the proposal submitted by the US Secretary of the Treasury, James Baker, at the IMF/World Bank annual conference held in Seoul (September 1985), which purports to open new ground for solving the Third World debt problem. Because it was hailed by the international financial community as being 'the solution' (although Third World countries, especially those of the Cartagena Group, have been very cautious about it) it is worth commenting on the Baker Plan (BP), as it has come to be known.

The main objectives and characteristics of the BP are: (a) to lend fresh capital to the 15 most indebted countries of the Third World, to a total amount of $29 billion ($20 billion from commercial banks and $9 billion from the World Bank and other multilateral credit organizations) during a three-year period; (b) in order to be considered as candidates for such help, governments must adopt a programme of further liberalization and privatization of their economies; in other words, the state should withdraw from all those activities that can be accomplished by the private sector (including, of course, US-based transnational corporations); (c) in addition, debtor nations would have to comply rigorously with the adjustment guidelines dictated by the IMF and the World Bank; (d) the emphasis of the BP lies on the need for economic growth in debtor countries, so that they can obtain the additional capital needed to make those indispensable imports required for reactivating investment and economic performance in general, especially in export activities; such a reactivation is seen as a precondition for increasing export earnings and facilitating punctual debt servicing; (e) a transfer of governmental enterprises and equity capital in different activities (including territorial possessions) could be considered as a mechanism for partial repayment of the debt.*

Apart from constituting a procedure to inject a tiny amount of fresh capital – a mere illusion, since this sum represents less than one-third of what just the Latin American 'beneficiaries' would have to pay as interest – the Baker Plan will be acting as a kind of Trojan horse for the introduction of a new philosophy of indebtedness with growth. In fact, what makes the BP sound somewhat attractive to debtor countries is that it recognizes that there must be economic growth of a sufficient magnitude to permit servicing the debt without further deterioration of living conditions in debtor nations. This has been hailed by many in Latin America as a demonstration of Mr Baker's sensitivity and realism. We feel, however, that behind Mr Baker's proposal there is the implicit recognition

---

*This last proposal had been made earlier by a number of bankers, the most representative being Preston Martin, Vice-Chairman of the US Federal Reserve Board. Statements he made in this regard gave rise to a notorious telephone incident with his superior at the Board, Paul Volcker (then in Japan) who dismissed the idea because it meant deviating from the strict application of IMF adjustment policies. Since then Mr Volcker seems to have changed his position, as he is now an enthusiastic supporter of the Baker Plan.

that it is not possible to continue squeezing Latin American and other Third World peoples for an indefinite period of time. At the heart of this recognition lies the profound fear that an excessive squeeze might lead to one of the following two situations: (i) a popular insurrection, which would mean not only the immediate suspension of all debt services but, still worse, the establishment of 'popular governments' that will most likely be 'unfriendly' to the US government; (ii) a more pacific, but no less dramatic decision by existing governments to declare themselves in default, in order to avoid the possible political upheavals of an insurrection. Pragmatic US politicians, including Mr Baker, realized that they could not run any of these risks. They, therefore, decided to apply the old economic lessons: if there is some economic growth the poor will have the chance of getting something or, at least, they will not lose hope of getting something; various industrial and commercial segments will be reactivated, hence imports and exports will increase, unemployment will tend to decrease; service payments will thus be less painful. That is, the best of all possible scenarios: economic reactivation with socio-political deactivation, plus punctual payment of debt interest.

The Baker Plan (which after more than one year had been applied only in Mexico) has been accompanied, however, by a hardening in the IMF and World Bank conditions. The central elements of this Plan follow the traditional 'carrot–and–stick' approach. The carrot is the sum of $10 billion a year in loans, at the moment when debtor nations are desperate for fresh capital; the stick is the obligation of recipient countries to open their economies further to foreign investment, to eliminate all import restrictions, as well as all export and domestic consumption subsidies. This would increase the debtors' vulnerability, as they would surely be facing the virtual annihilation of their own industrial base. In the case of those countries that are cereal exporters (Argentina and Uruguay, for example), they would have to face the fierce competition of huge US grain surpluses.

It is not surprising, therefore, that Latin American nations have so far been reluctant to request their incorporation into the Baker's Club! One exception is the latest renegotiation of the Mexican debt, a lengthy and most difficult exercise that was concluded in November 1986, whereby a package of $12 billion in loans was approved (half to be granted by multilateral agencies and the other half by a large consortium of commercial banks), with a grace period of 20 years to repay the principal. An important clause of this package links the process of loan disbursement to variations in oil prices: if prices fall to a level below $9 per barrel, additional loans will automatically be granted; conversely, if prices rise to a level above $14 per barrel, the amounts to be disbursed would diminish. Although such linkage does not in itself help in solving Mexico's external burden, as export losses would be 'compensated for' by further indebtedness, it nevertheless constitutes a step towards recognition that the relationship Commodity Prices/Interest Rates and Payments is crucial to debtor nations. Another important element in the package was the reduction in the surchage over and above the LIBOR interest rate, from around two percentage points to less than one point.

On the other hand, it is difficult to understand what would qualitatively differentiate the situation that might be generated by the BP from that experienced during the 1970s when capital inflow from commercial banks was ample enough and economic growth rates were high but the degree of indebtedness reached record levels. If the process that took place between 1975 and 1981 led to the catastrophic situation of the last four years, we fail to see how an increment in borrowing by Latin America as postulated by the BP would take the most indebted nations out of that situation.

There is a more 'compassionate' initiative, from US Congressman Bradley (Democrat), that is beginning to be seriously considered. The 'Bradley Plan' proposes the slashing of $57 billion from the debt of the poorest Third World nations (thus cancelling the entire debt in the case of many of them), and diminishing the interest rates applied to the remaining countries by three percentage points. This initiative, submitted in early 1986, had not received much attention until November, when the Democrat Party recovered the full control of the Senate and reinforced their control of the House of Representatives. The Bradley proposal has now gained centre-stage and, for the first time ever, the US Congress will be considering in earnest the Third World debt problem. A special meeting on this subject was convened for early December 1986, and it is most likely that other special sessions or hearings will follow in the course of 1987.

Although Congressman Bradley's initiative (whose full details have not been disclosed so far) is on a more correct track than the Baker Plan, we believe that it is still quite distant from tackling the Third World debt issue in a comprehensive way. A more appropriate approach to the debt problem, in the case of Latin America, should include, in our view, the concept of *legitimacy* of the debt, as was proclaimed by President Alfonsín of Argentina during his electoral campaign (but abandoned after the election). The inclusion of such a concept would entail at least the following steps.

1. Deflation of the debt to its legitimate size through: (i) discounting of all artificial increments in the international rates of interest over and above a basic rate of six per cent per year, from 1976 onwards; (ii) a compensation for the drop in raw material prices since 1980, which has mostly favoured the industrialized economies.

2. Repatriation of all capital that flew away from Latin America since 1976 in various forms and schemes;

3. For the remainder of the debt, the following conditions should also be applied: (i) transformation of the monetary value of such debt into its equivalent in raw materials and/or manufactured products; to that end, reasonable unit prices should be used; (ii) a maximum yearly rate of interest of six per cent; (iii) a 25–year period for repayment of the principal; (iv) stability of commodity unit prices throughout the whole repayment period.

4. No new loans (excepting short-term credit for trade purposes) nor debt

re-negotiation or roll-overs would be requested throughout the repayment period.

Let us examine these proposals in more detail.

Deflation of the debt

It can be roughly estimated that Latin American countries have paid out over $100 billion during the last ten years on account of excessive interest rates. If we apply a differential of four per cent (ten minus six per cent) to the outstanding debt throughout the 1976–1985 period, we reach a figure of around $105–110 billion.* This is a sum that Latin America does not owe and that it should not recognize as legitimate, since it originated exclusively in the monetary and financial problems of industrial nations, mainly the US. Had the interest rates remained at their 1975–6 levels, the Latin American countries would not have faced the huge payments they had to make during the following years, and therefore their need to borrow would have been much smaller.

If, at the same time, prices of raw materials had stayed at their 1980 levels, export earnings would have been some $25–30 billion higher than they actually were; had this been the case, Latin America's borrowing needs would have declined by the same amount.

Adding the above figures we reach a total of some $130–140 billion, which corresponds to about one-third the total present Latin American debt. In any serious negotiations with the creditors this amount should be deducted from the principal, which would thus be reduced to around $260 billion.

In terms of physical resources, such 'deflation' of the principal would represent a diminution of around 680 million MAPRALs (at 1983 prices or close to one billion MAPRALs at 1986 prices.† That is, Latin America would be retaining, for its own future consumption or utilization, an impressive amount of physical resources, that today go to benefit the creditor nations.

The flight of capital

As indicated earlier, it is estimated that not less than $130–150 billion left the region as capital flight in the course of the last ten years alone. These are savings generated within the region, which left it as a consequence mainly of the very unequal wealth and income distribution patterns prevailing in

---

*These are purely indicative figures. More precise calculations would have to take into consideration not only the detailed annual variations, but also those loans from governments and multilateral credit institutions at usually lower rates. It must also be borne in mind that interest rates were for several years well above ten per cent.

†As explained in Chapter One the MAPRAL is equivalent to one metric ton of the package of 18 important Latin American raw materials.

Latin American countries. It is not the industrial worker, or the peasant, or the white-collar worker who buys dollars to open accounts or acquire real estate abroad; it is the relatively small group of people benefiting from existing economic and political systems who send their money away. Sharply skewed wealth/income distribution schemes and high rates of profit permit the capitalist class, with only a fraction of the appropriated economic surplus, to continue running their domestic operations profitably, while sending abroad a large proportion of that surplus. In other words, as was noted earlier, a very important fraction of total internal savings is continuously transferred abroad.

It is clear that such a process is also directly responsible for the increase in Latin America's indebtedness. Had those savings remained within the region, the need to borrow would have decreased by the same proportion. Since such monies are deposited or invested mostly in creditor countries, strongly helping their economies, it does not seem logical, nor just, that Latin Americans should pay interest on them. Instead, it would be fair to pursue an agreement between debtor and creditor institutions and governments to repatriate the capital. By means of special extradition procedures, owners of those capital assets abroad would have the opportunity of returning them to their places of origin, and converting them into national currencies for investment locally in activities of social interest, subject, of course, to the laws, regulations and fiscal charges prevailing in the respective countries of Latin America. There is no reason whatsoever why 'an appropriate climate of confidence' should be established in order to promote the return of such fugitive capital, as certain groups in the US and in Latin America request as a prior condition. This would simply mean reinforcing already existing advantages in terms of higher profit rates, lower taxes and salaries, etc., and of course, the broadening of the income gap between different social groups. There would be no guarantee anyway that the increased capital would not flee once more as soon as clouds gather in the economic skies of the Latin American countries.

If a repatriation process gets under way, debtor countries could apply the foreign currency thus recovered to the repayment of the principal. If we assume, conservatively, that the amount to be repatriated under such scheme is in the order of $125 billion, this would mean that another third of the standing debt is slashed from the present bill.

In physical terms, this would represent the retention on Latin American soil of resources amounting to another 650 million MAPRALs (1983 prices) or 950 million if 1986 prices are considered. Adding together figures under our first two headings, we arrive at a huge volume of resources – over 1.3 billion MAPRALs (1983) or nearly 2 billion (1986) – that would remain in the region. But the total real recuperation of resources would be much higher, as all the interest saved should be added. Assuming an average interest rate of ten per cent, and no amortization of the principal, in 20 years those volumes would have trebled: 3.9 billion MAPRALs at 1983 prices (1.3 billion for principal and 2.6 billion for interest saved), and 6 billion MAPRALs at 1986 prices (2 billion for principal and 4 billion for interest saved).

Payment of 'legitimate' principal
With the reductions estimated above, we arrive at a net figure of some $135 billion. This might be considered the legitimate portion of the debt, notwithstanding the fact that even this reduced fraction contains some elements of illegitimacy (such as all those superfluous imports made by Latin American nations, which undoubtedly favour the economies of creditor countries). If the legitimate debt is paid in 25 years, with an annual interest rate of not more than six per cent, the total service would amount to $1.35 billion in the first year, and $5.7 billion in the final year. These figures seem to be manageable even in a situation such as the present one of economic stress in Latin America. The other condition is that annual services be converted into a basket of selected raw materials at prices that are fixed beforehand (for example 1980 prices). Otherwise, through further price manipulation and depreciation creditor countries could well extract the same or similar volumes of basic resources, even after the debt has been deflated to one-third its original (present) size. In terms of physical resources, the above solution would represent an initial outflow of 62 million MAPRALs (1980 prices) or 70 million (1983 prices), and only 27 to 30 million in the final year. The accumulated outflow during the 25–year period would fluctuate between 1.1 and 1.25 billion MAPRALs according to the unit price of the MAPRAL adopted.

With such a solution, Latin American countries would not require further borrowing to repay the debt, nor would they have to force their exports of all kinds of goods in order to service such a debt. By just devoting an average of ten to twelve per cent of their present export earnings they could see the burden of their foreign debt disappear.

The above figures should be contrasted with those that result from a continuation of the present size of the debt and interest rates. Assuming, as previously, that no new debts are contracted but that no amortization on the present one is made either, the total outflow of resources during a 25–year period, for interest payment alone, would be of 4.6 billion MAPRALs (1980 prices) or 5.2 billion MAPRALs (1983 prices); were the present oil and other raw materials prices to remain unaltered, that is, with the MAPRAL unit price at about 130 dollars, the total remittance for interest payment would skyrocket to 7.7 billion MAPRALs during the 25–year period considered, at the end of which the original debt would have remained intact. The difference between these figures and those resulting from the application of a formula such as the one we have suggested, should be regarded as the net despoliation of Latin American resources by creditor nations in the North.

Needless to insist, the methodology we are suggesting should be tailored to the circumstances that are peculiar to each individual Latin American nation. There are differences in the composition of the export basket, probably also in the price behaviour of each component of those baskets, as well as possible differences in the rates of interest at which each nation has contracted its various loans, all of which should be considered carefully during the negotiation process. What is important, however, is that the principles of 'debt deflation' and 'indexation' (raw materials prices/rates of interest) are strictly kept for each country. It should be clearly understood, therefore, that notwithstanding the technical complexities of the proposed negotiations scheme, which will require the participation of many experts from both creditor and debtor nations, and from multilateral organizations as well, the main focus of those negotiations is of a political nature.

Beyond dependency: elimination of the structural causes of indebtedness

The adoption of a scheme such as the one depicted above would represent a gigantic step towards the diminution of economic dependency. Decisions on what and how much to export and import would not be dictated any more by the obligation of meeting high foreign financial commitments, but mainly by real national development interests. However, to gain *real* economic and political independence it is essential that the deep causes leading to the indebtedness process be totally eradicated, and that the present situation of financial, commercial, technological and cultural dependency be radically transformed. If basic patterns of social behaviour – which currently entail high waste and high import co-efficients – are not modified, the outflow of resources, even if it may be substantially diminished at the beginning, will most probably increase once again.

As long as the way in which countries in the South relate to those in the industrial North remains intact, and the development philosophy does not change, Southern nations will continue to be easy prey for cultural penetration from the North, hence of lifestyles that prevail in Northern industrial countries. It becomes indispensable, therefore, to start a delinking process that allows Southern nations to achieve a high degree of national and regional autonomy and self-sufficiency, and, more important still, to achieve a more advanced stage in the path towards a rationally ordered society. Dieter Senghaas, in an article written just a few years ago,[79] stated very clearly what he calls 'the imperative of dissociation', which constitutes in his view one of the fundamental imperatives for Third World development.

> In the long run, the Third World has a chance of building up self-reliant and viable economies and societies only if it dissociates itself temporarily from the prevailing international economy, i.e. the metropolitan economies... Historical experience of capitalistic *and* socialistic development processes that resulted in

more or less viable structures shows that without a period of self-centredness, the duration of which may vary from case to case, i.e. *without protection motivated by development policy, an intensive* (as opposed to an extensive) *development of productive forces is hardly possible* . . . And is it just coincidence or of more fundamental significance that in an area of western and central Europe in which the development processes of our modern age began, development was determined by "temporary severance from the main arteries of previously prevailing trade"? . . . Trade must be pursued *selectively*, and only that form of *selective cooperation* should be practised which benefits the building up of a viable internal structure in the countries of the southern continents. Hence, what is involved . . . is calculated isolation coupled with selective utilization of the world market . . . For the majority of countries of the Third World, *dissociation* nowadays means in particular: a break with the traditional, export-oriented economy and instead mobilization of their *own* resources with the goal of making such resources utilizable for their *own* purposes (original emphasis).

Whatever the word – disconnection, dissociation, or de-linking – the issue, as Senghaas very well indicates, is basically that of achieving a much higher degree of autonomy; this means acquiring less and less from the US, Europe, Japan, or even the USSR. Be they machines for peace or for war, be it technology for the production or utilization of those machines, be they intermediate or finished goods, including foodstuffs, the key to the de-linking process lies in the progressive shrinking of commercial ties with the Northern industrial powers.

As replacement of material goods is postponed, for example through longer utilization periods, better equipment maintenance, repair of things rather than simply discarding them; as excessive and superfluous or dispensable material consumption is reduced, and ultimately eliminated, the demand for imported goods and services will automatically diminish. Hence, Third World autonomy will tend to increase. If an anti-wastage conscience is promoted among different population groups, particularly among the waste-prone richer ones, there is no doubt that substantial portions of current imports could well be wiped out. As we have already stated, it is neither possible, nor desirable – it would indeed be absurd – to 'democratize' the excessive consumption patterns of a minority that is permanently trying to imitate the 'American way of life'. Firstly, this is because what is consumed over and above that which is necessary for a reasonable or decent standard of living is pure waste; secondly, because in any case there would not be enough for everybody, particularly if in this term 'everybody' we include not only the present population of the world but future generations as well.

What should be democratized instead is an equitable and rational behaviour pattern, that would imply not only renouncing the exploitation of other human beings but also the thoughtless exploitation of nature. This would necessarily imply a drastic recomposition in demand and supply of goods and services. The present emphasis on the production and consumption of superfluous, noxious or luxurious goods would have to give way to an increase in the production and consumption of those essential goods and services that large segments of Southern populations are lacking today. Because of their useless nature, many activities that are characteristic of capitalist 'developed' societies would have to be suppressed, but many others would have to be created, in the areas of science, culture, recreation, sports and similar activities. Human toil would be rewarded according to the effort made and not to the whimsical demand of rich minorities. Both responsibilities and benefits would be democratized. If the total quantity of work needed to produce the overall mass of goods and services required by the community turns out to be lower than the total availability of human labour power – given a certain technological level – then free time should be equitably shared. Contrary to what happens today, in a rationally ordered society there would be no reason why some people should overwork while others have to face forced unemployment.

Human relations, because they would be less competitive in the search for a source of income, or in the pursuit of a higher income, would tend to be more communal. Solidarity would stimulate the creation of workers' cooperative organizations, for the production, transportation, processing, and distribution of essential goods and services. The size of such organizations would be adapted to prevailing conditions in each instance and not to the requirements posed by the need to obtain a given rate of profit. Craftsmen, workers and peasants could reach appropriate understandings and arrangements for the exchange of their respective outputs, without having to rely on the participation of intermediaries who absorb the highest proportion of the total benefit. It would be a society where the concept of sharing would prevail over those of hoarding, speculating, exploiting and oppressing. It would be a more frugal and rational society, albeit without losing its creativity and ingenuity.

An initial step on the road towards a rationally ordered society – which would help to solve the foreign debt problem and the political and economic dependence associated with it – could be the compression of imports made from industrial nations to a minimum compatible with the true requirements posed by rational behaviour patterns. Most essential goods and services are of a simple nature, and can be easily produced domestically or within the region with the resources and technologies that are available. Supplies of food, clothing, housing, transport, education, health services, recreation and culture do not need to depend on inputs from the industrialized world. Latin American countries are in a position to develop suitable capital-goods industries that can produce both the machines that will process the Latin American raw materials and the finished essential goods that are required. By eliminating the superfluous portion of consumption, the need to import will be significantly reduced. If, in addition, an aggressive import substitution policy is pursued, as was the case a few decades ago, Latin America could become economically self-sufficient and politically sovereign. In such a situation, the need to count upon large quantities of hard currency would disappear, since dollars, marks, yen, and so on would be required for relatively few selected operations; this would, therefore, exempt these countries from the obligation to borrow for their development and, consequently, from the compulsion to transfer their physical resources by way of exports. By not borrowing and not having to pay interest and other charges, these countries would not only avoid the juggling of the US (or European, or Japanese) financial and fiscal administration, but, even more important, they would be able to retain for their own benefit the fruits of Latin American work.

With decreasing needs for foreign currency to pay for imports, the imperative to export will decline accordingly. Thus, domestic (national and regional) resources will primarily serve to fill present gaps in socially-needed goods and services, as well as to sustain future generations adequately.

The demand for increasingly sophisticated technologies will also have to diminish, since the urge to participate in a growingly competitive international market will have decreased. Thus, today's fear of lagging behind – which is quite common among techno-bureaucrats of different political views, and among entrepreneurs and professionals in general – will also disappear. Equally important, the present Latin American fear of challenging creditor institutions and governments to force them to enter into an equitable debt negotiation process will disappear as well.

Were creditor institutions and governments to refuse this challenge Latin American countries could very well default on their debts; their essential import needs would be covered by intra- and inter-regional exchanges. All this would necessarily mean an acceleration in the de-linking process, with great advantages for Latin American countries.

It is doubtful, however, that the North will come to accept the risks of a global Latin American default. The preservation of the international financial system's security depends on the avoidance of such a collective payments shut-down. We believe, therefore, that Latin American countries are in an excellent position – if they act unitedly – to enforce conditions and negotiating terms such as deflation of principal, lower interest rates, capital repatriation, and indexation. With a social transformation scheme such as that suggested above, Latin America's bargaining position would be very strong.

Simplified production processes, as a result of demand 'essentialization', will have important implications also for the size and locality of human organizations and institutions. For unknown reasons dinosaurs disappeared from Earth about 65 million years ago; they reappeared during the 20th Century in the form of megalopolises, transnational corporations, industrial and commercial conglomerates, hypermarkets, skyscrapers, and so on. However, they will have to disappear once again, to give way to activities that are in agreement with new social values. With a pattern of consumption that is much simpler, its satisfaction will require techniques that are also simpler and less demanding in terms of production scales. It would be possible to undertake the urgent tasks of economic and demographic decentralization successfully. A society opting for non-contamination and non-poisoning will tend to use new ways of producing food (which, in fact, are very old). An example is the system called *organic* or *alternative* agriculture.* By doing so, society will be able to rediscover the wisdom of peasants – for whom conservation of soil and water have always been central elements to their survival – to apply it in the production of food and fibres needed by the urban population. This does not mean, of course, that it will be necessary or inevitable, under such a new conception, to forget or put aside all useful knowledge gained from modern science and technology.

It might be said, perhaps, that the slackening of the commodity flow from South to North would strengthen and accelerate the process of substitution for resources that are more readily available within the North itself. But in fact such a substitution process has been taking place for a long time, and has accelerated considerably during the last few years.

For example, the Japanese have been producing at the experimental level – apparently with great success – very hard ceramic materials that can replace various metals, including those used in car engines. Advances in bio-engineering in the US open the possibility that many articles that the North is forced to import may one day be produced locally with domestic resources. Biologists now consider living organisms as being things that absorb and store information, and modify their behaviour as a result of that information.[81] Living organisms are self-programmed; it is possible, therefore, to re-programme them and thus obtain living beings that are different from the original ones. Marriage between computers and living tissues could give rise to a totally different kind of world economy, which will be based almost exclusively on bio-engineering enterprises.[82]

The first phase of bio-technology is already mature as scientists progressively know more about how to modify genes and transfer them from one living organism to another, thus transforming the specific characteristics of such organisms.

An understanding of the cybernetic relationship between gene, cell, organism,

---

*Altieri[80] defines traditional and organic agriculture as follows. *Traditional agriculture* is that characterized by crop diversification or polculture, both in time and space; it is a traditional strategy to promote diet variety, output stability, risk minimization, diminished incidence of plant diseases and insect damage, an efficient use of manpower and maximization of economic returns with low technology. *Organic agriculture* is a production system which rests to the maximum possible extent on the following elements: crop rotation; crop residues; animal, vegetable and green manures; organic waste from outside the farm; mechanical cultivation; mineral rock, and biological control of pests. All this is required to maintain productivity of soil and crops, to provide plants with needed nutrients, and to control insects, weeds and other pests. Organic farmers avoid – or restrict as much as possible – the use of synthetic fertilizers, pesticides, growth regulators, and additives in animal feeding.

and environment will lay the basis for the second stage of the age of biotechnology. At this stage, scientists will be able to expand beyond the engineering of genetic characteristics and begin applying engineering design to the construction of entire organisms ... stage three is the engineering of entire ecosystems.[83]

At present, experiments are being carried out with the development of micro-organisms that can 'eat' metals such as cobalt, iron, nickel and manganese, or bacteria which, if injected into low-grade mineral ores, produce an enzyme that 'eats' the ores' salts leaving copper – or other metals – in an almost pure state. These 'glutton' organisms will provide an easier and more economical way of extracting metals. From the point of view of industrial nations this would be a liberation from the dependence they suffer concerning supply sources for these and other materials. This would also mean that the total volume of exploitable mineral reserves would be greatly increased, notwithstanding the fact that the total resource base will continue to be the same.

One could well imagine, therefore, that at a certain point the de-linking process may be initiated by the Northern countries themselves. Such a decision will probably be taken on the basis of what for them is easiest and cheapest: either to secure – in whatever way – the resources located in the South, or to liberate themselves through technology.

Southern countries have nothing to lose if dissociation takes place, except for the binding link to a wasteful and destructive consumption-production model and to the forces that design and manipulate such a model. Latin American countries together have practically all the basic resources they need to sustain their populations at a reasonable level of well-being, granted that the size of those populations does not continue growing indefinitely. Note that we are thinking in terms of a high degree of regional self-sufficiency, which can be even higher if it is extended to cover the whole of the Third World. There should be intra-regional and inter-regional exchange flows, based on barter and other similar ad hoc mechanisms, adapted to the conditions and requirements of these countries, at the same level in relative but not in absolute terms as current trade with industrialized nations. In absolute terms, international trade should diminish once wastage in consumption and production has been eradicated.

The liberation from 'trade fetishism' will have to be one of the distinctive features of the qualitative changes to take place in a new society. Such fetishism is deeply rooted in the developmentalist philosophy that has prevailed in Latin America during the last several decades, placing foreign trade and net capital inflow amongst its fundamental pillars. But, as we have seen, such development has not only widened the gap in living standards betwen social groups, but has also led to the situation of extreme dependency in which Latin America finds itself today. It has contributed to the accelerated flight of resources towards the imperial metropolis and has furthermore contributed to the environment's severe deterioration.

The dissociation of the South implies, therefore, the disconnection from a lifestyle that favours waste, injustice, hypocrisy and ostentation. It also implies breaking with a false notion of progress, as such 'progress' results in a deterioration in the quality of life of vast numbers of human beings, as well as implying dissociation from cultural patterns that favour quantity over quality. It is not, therefore, simply an economic or commercial matter, nor merely a confrontation between two blocs, the one very powerful and the other very weak. In essence, it is a new way of understanding human relations, among themselves and with the ecosystem of which humans form a part. It is urgent that Latin American countries, pressed by the imperative need to bring about real solutions to their problems of maldevelopment, finally decide to make a lateral jump instead of continuing to push for more of the same.

Dissociation of Latin American countries, and eventually of other Third World nations, will inevitably provoke different types of reactions in the countries of the North. On the one hand, these will lose an important market for the disposal of their manufacturing, agricultural and financial surpluses; on the other hand, they will also lose access to cheap sources for the supply of strategic materials. The combination of both factors will result in a general increase in the cost of the ostentatious and wasteful living standards of Northern societies. There will be less of those who, in these societies, may continue keeping such opulent consumption levels, while there will be more of those unable to have access to the fruits of a prosperity that seemed to be unlimited. Such new circumstances will undoubtedly provoke a regressive income redistribution; the gap between the haves and the have-nots and the resulting friction among them will tend to increase. Moreover, the gaps within the have-nots will also widen: between those who can get and keep a remunerated job, and those who lose their employment or who cannot enter the job market. At the same time, the inter-imperialist conflict will become sharper and stronger. It is likely that all of this will contribute to accelerating the process of deterioration and disintegration of the current social system of the industrialized economies.

It is possible that dominant groups in the North will try to impede Southern dissociation, since it would seriously menace the functioning of their economies and the foundations of their so jealously guarded lifestyles. They might opt for the classical military solution, or, in combination with this, the covert or overt stimulation of subversion within Southern countries and even military conflicts between them. Thus, the North would not only attempt the establishment of puppet regimes that are in favour of a continuation of the dependent status quo, but would obstruct the consolidation of a united Latin American front (something that is obvious in the extreme difficulty of forming a debtors' club in Latin America).

At the same time, however, the attempt in the South to initiate a serious social transformation process that will lead towards a rationally ordered society and to the growing dissociation from the North, will undoubtedly provoke a strengthening of those groups in the North itself that are pugnaciously fighting for a change in the lifestyles prevalent in their own societies. Military action – overt or covert – designed to suppress Southern attempts to liberate themselves from consumerism's oppression and eliminate the aberration of social wastage, would be strongly resisted by those groups, probably more vigorously still than the popular rejection in the US of the Vietnam war, or the anti-nuclear demonstrations in Europe. Besides, we sincerely believe that many leaders in Northern nations will finally understand that indefinite economic growth policies – at whatever cost – will inevitably lead to the collective suicide of the human species. We trust, therefore, that a liberating movement starting in the South, towards that gigantic lateral leap, will have positive effects for the whole of humanity.

We have covered a great distance: we started with the consideration of a phenomenon that might be seen as occasional and temporary – the external debt – to conclude by questioning the present forms of social organization. We believe that until the veils that conceal the true roots of the debasement and misery of our societies are lifted; until the rusty analytical tools that are currently used to approach economic, social and political problems are abandoned; until many of the premises and fetishes that serve as a reference framework in carrying out such analysis are thrown overboard, it will truly be difficult, if not impossible, to attempt a change in values that could lead to the rationally ordered society which, we think, is the only option left to change the progressively Frankensteinian nature of present societies.

References

1. In this book we use the terms Centre-Periphery and North-South interchangeably.

2. For a more complete analysis of this process see: J.P. Lewis, 'Can We Escape the Path of Mutual Injury?,' in *US Foreign Policy and the Third World, Agenda 1983* (Overseas Development Council, Washington DC, 1983).

3. Ibid.

4. J.C. Sanchez-Arnau (ed.) *Debt and Development*, (Praeger, New York, 1982) Ch. 1.

5. G. Corm, 'The Indebtedness of the Developing Countries: Origins and Mechanisms', in J.C. Sanchez-Arnau (ed.), *Debt and Development*.

6. H. van B. Cleveland and W.H. Bruce-Brittain, 'Are the LDCs in Over their Heads?', *Foreign Affairs,* July 1977.

7. P. Dhonte, *Clockwork Debt* (D.C. Heath, Canada, 1979).

8. O. Beim, Rescuing the LDC's, *Foreign Affairs,* July 1977.

9. Chennery and Strout, Foreign Assistance and Economic Development, quoted in Dhonte. *Clockwork Debt.*

10. Dhonete, *Clockwork Debt.*

11. CEPAL, *La crisis en América Latina: su evaluación y perspectivas* (Doc. E/CEPAL/G. 1294, 9 February 1984).

12. M. Motfitt, *The World's Money* (Simon and Schuster, New York, 1983).

13. R. Green, 'La deuda externa del Gobierno Mexicano' in N. Lustig (ed.) *Panorama y perspectivas de la economía mexicana* (El Colegio de México, México, 1980).

14. Dhonte, *Clockwork Debt.*

15. Introduction to the Report of the Overseas Development Council 1983.

16. Abraham F. Lowenthal, 'Latin America and the Caribbean: Towards a New U.S. Policy', in Overseas Development Council 1983 report.

17. Report of the Independent Commission on International Development Problems, presided over by Willy Brandt *Norte-Sur, Un Programa para la Supervivencia, (North-South, A Programme for Survival),* (Editorial Pluma, Bogotá, 1980).

18. Corm, in *Debt and Development.*

19. A good part of the information presented in this section has been taken from C. Payer, *The Debt Trap* (Monthly Review Press, New York, 1974).

20. S. Pineda, Brazil correspondent, *Excelsior,* 10 October 1984.

21. *Time*, no. 27, 2 July 1984.

22. R.W. Feinberg, 'Bridging the Crisis: The World Bank and the U.S. interests in the 1980s', in Overseas Development Council, 1983 report.

23. World Bank, 1985 Report.

24. For a detailed account of what happened during this interesting period, see Moffitt, *The World's Money*.

25. *Time*, no. 27, 2 July 1984.

26. *Excelsior*, 12 July 1984.

27. Interview by A. Berdejo, published in several parts in May and June, 1984. The section quoted here appeared on 2 June 1984.

28. *Excelsior*, 12 July 1984.

29. *Excelsior*, 17 February 1984.

30. E. Daly (ed.), *Towards A Steady-State Economy*.

31. The African examples were taken from 'Women in Food Production, Food Handling and Nutrition', a study prepared under the auspices of the Protein-Calorie Advisory Group of the UN (PAG), in *Food and Nutrition Paper no. 8*, UN Food and Agricultural Organization (FAO) Rome, 1979).

32. F. Fajnzylber, *La industrialización trunca de America Latina*, (Editorial Nueva Imagen, México, 1983).

33. C. Schatan, 'La estructura del desecuilibrio comercial, 1975–80', *Economía Mexicana*, Departamento de Economía, Centro de Investigación y Docencia Económica, A.C., vol. 3, October 1983, Mexico.

34. J.A. Hobson, quoted by G.A. Smith 'The Teleological View of Wealth', in H.E. Daley (ed.), *Towards a Steady-State Economy*.

35. J. Schatan, 'El "Derecho a la Alimentación" versus las "Libertad para Escoger"', ('The "right to food" vs. the "freedom to choose"') *Revista Interamericana de Planificación*, Inter-American Planning Society (SIAP), vol. XVII, no. 66, June 1983.

36. M. Godelier, *Racionalidad e Irracionalidad en Economía*, Siglo XXI, 1982, Mexico.

37. P.A. Baran, *The Political Economy of Growth* (Monthly Review Press, New York, 1957).

38. Data obtained from surveys carried out by the National Nutrition Institute (INN) and from the National Survey on Income and Expenditure at the Household Level, Ministry of Planning (SPP), 1977.

39. I. Restrepo and D. Phillips, *La basura en el Distrito Federal* (Centro de Ecodesarrollo, Mexico, 1982).

40. J. Schatan, 'El abastecimiento de alimentos en la ciudad de México', mimeo; document prepared for the Program PROCADES/CEPAL, UN, Mexico, September 1982.

41. F. Moore Lappé and J. Collins, *Food First* (Ballantine, New York, 1979).

42. *Time*, 10 May 1982.

43. *New York Times*, 30 September 1984.

44. *New York Times*, 3 October 1984.

45. *Excelsior*, 10 July 1984.

46. R.A. Caro, *The years of Lyndon Johnson: The Path to Power* (Knopf, New York, 1982).

47. D. Ogilvy, *Ogilvy on Advertising* (Crown, New York, 1983).

48. UN, *Desarme* (Disarmament) vol. VI, no. 3, Autumn/Winter 1983.

49. J. Wilheim, 'Metropolización y Medio Ambiente', in O. Sunkel and N. Gligo (eds.) *Estilos de Desarrollo y Medio Ambiente en la América Latina* (Fondo de Cultura, Mexico 1980).

50. H. Durán de la Fuente, 'Estilos de Desarrollo de la industria manufacturera

y madio ambiente en la América Latina', in O. Sunkel and N. Gligo (eds.) *Estilos*.

51. J.M. Nava, US correspondent in *Excelsior* 10 November 1984.

52. L. Kowarick, 'El precio del progreso: crecimiento económico, expoliación urbana y la cuestión del medio ambiente', in *Estilos*.

53. A. Uribe and F. Szekely, 'Localización y Tecnología Industrial en la América Latina y sus efectos en el Medio Ambiente', in *Estilos*.

54. J. Trénova, 'Perspectivas de la energía solar como sucedánea del petróleo en América Latina hasta el año 2000', in *Estilos*.

55. I. Vergara in, 'El problema de la contaminación marina producido por el transporte marítimo en la América Latina', in *Estilos* estimates that in recent years tankers in the Latin-American region have discharged in the sea an average of around 140 thousand tons of fuels per annum. If other contaminating sources are added a figure of over half a million tons is reached.

56. D. Weir and M. Schapiro, *Círculo de Veneno: los plaguicidas y el hambre en un mundo hambriento* (Editorial Terra Nova, Mexico, 1982).

57. Information from *Sos ecologico*, a publication of the Ecological Group, University of Tolima, Ibagué, Colombia, February 1978.

58. ibid., July

59. N. Gligo and J. Morello, 'Notas sobre la historia ecológica de la América Latina', in *Estilos*.

60. T. Halperin, quoted by Gligo and Morello in *Estilos*.

61. P. Harrison, *Inside the Third World*, (Penguin, Harmondsworth, 1981).

62. J. Wilheim, *Metropolización y Medio Ambiente*.

63. P. Cloud, 'Mineral Resources in Fact and Fancy,' in H.E. Daly (ed.), *Towards a Steady-State Economy*.

64. US Bureau of Mines, *Mineral Facts and Problems, 1975*, quoted in *Resources, Society and the Future*, Secretariat for Futures Studies, Stockholm, Sweden (Pergamon Press, 1980).

65. J.E. Tilton, *The future of Non-Fuel Minerals* (The Brookings Institution, Washington DC, 1977) table 2–3.

66. *Excelsior*, 28 June 1984.

67. R.J. Barnet, *The Lean Years: Politics in the Age of Scarcity* (Simon and Schuster, New York, 1980).

68. Barnet, ibid.

69. L. Thurow, 'The Implications of Zero Economic Growth', in Joint Economic Committee of Congress, *US Prospects for Growth*, (Washington DC, 1976).

70. A. Herrera et al., *Catastrophe or New Society? A Latin America World Model*, a project carried out by a team of the Bariloche Foundation, Buenos Aires, Argentina (International Development Research Center of the Government of Canada, Ottawa, Canada, 1976).

71. J. Rifkin with T. Howard, *Entropy* (The Viking Press, New York, 1980).

72. E. Leff, Racionalidad ecotecnológica y manejo integrado de recursos', in *Revista Interamericana de Planificación*, SIAP, vol. XVIII, no. 69, March 1984.

73. Rifkin and Howard, *Entropy*.

74. J. Schatan, *The 'right to food' vs. the 'freedom to choose'*.

75. J.M. Culbertson, *Economic Development: An Ecological Approach*, (Knopf, New York, 1971).

76. J. Ellul, *Propaganda* (Vintage Books, New York, 1973).

77. G.N. Gordon, *Persuasion*, (Hastings House, New York, 1971).

78. Ellul, *Propaganda*.

79. D. Senghaas, 'The Case of Autarchy', *Development*, journal of the Society for International Development (SID), nos. 2 and 3.

80. M. Altieri. *Agroecology, The Scientific Basis of Alternative Agriculture* (University of California, Berkeley, 1983).

81. W.H. Thorpe quoted by J.Rifkin, *Algeny* (Viking Press, New York, 1983).

82. Rifkin, *Algeny*.

83. Rifkin, *Algeny*.

Index

advertising and consumption 2, 72-3, 100-4
Alfonsín, President 109
Argentina 85; arms purchases 74; growth of debt 5, 10, 12-13; and IMF 37; responsibility for debt 45-6, 48, 49
armaments imports 27, 48, 73-4, 83

Baker, James (Baker Plan) 106-9
balance of payments 13-15
Bariloche Group 96-8
bio-technology 117-18
Bolivia, 37, 105
Bradley, Congressman (Bradley Plan) 109
Brandt Commission report 30-1
Brazil 19, 37, 82, 85, 89; arms purchases 74; growth of debt 10, 12-13; imports 70-2, 76, 81; and IMF 37; responsibility for debt 45-6, 50
Bretton Woods Conference 32-4

capital flight 7, 27-8, 36, 45-51, 110-12
Cartagena Group 94, 104-7
Carter, Jimmy 39
Castro, Fidel 105
CEPAL see United Nations
Chile 16, 27, 82, 105; arms purchases 74; growth of debt 10, 12-13; imports 70-2, 77-9; responsibility for debt 45-6
China, People's Republic of 67-8
Colombia 46
commerical banks 9-11, 15, 26, 29-30
commercial loans (non-concessional) 9-11
commodity prices 6, 16, 109-10; falls in 18-23, 27, 41, 62, 90n; and interest rates 3, 7-8, 41-3, 106, 108, 113
concessional loans 9-10, 15-16
corruption 7, 28, 48-51
Costa Rica 46, 50, 87n
Cuba 10
cultural penetration by US 2

debt-export ratio 11-12

deforestation 88-9
de-linking of Third World 4, 113-20
demographic growth 95-6
desertification 88
'dollarization' 27

ecological considerations 2, 23-4, 61-2, 84-9, 104
ECLA see United Nations
El Salvador 46
entropy 99
exchange rates 36
export-led growth 1-2, 6

Fanon, Frantz: The Wretched of the Earth 100
free market system 55-6, 99-100
Friedman, Milton 99

García, President 105
gold price 39-40
gold standard 33
Gramm-Rudman Act (US) 40n
Great Depression 33
Green Party (West Germany) 104
gross national product (GNP): debt as proportion of 8, 12-13, interest payments as proportion of 10; projection for Latin America 97-8
Guatemala 46

Honduras 46
Hunt family 39-40

import substitution 6, 34
import of superfluous goods 2-3, 27, 36-7, 50-4, 70-3
inflation 7, 27, 39, 41
interdependence 31-2
interest rates 109-10; and commodity prices 3, 22, 41-3, 106, 108, 113; on concessional/non-concessional loans 9-

10; domestic/international 26-7; and export earnings 14-15, 26; and inflation 7; as proportion of GNP 10; variable 7, 39-41
International Bank for Reconstruction and Development (IBRD) *see* World Bank
International Monetary Fund (IMF) 6, 25, 33-4; adjustment policies 32, 34-8, 107, 108
India 72-3, 80-2
industrialized countries and Latin-American market 29-31
industry and external deficit 53-4
invoicing, under/over 49-50

legitimacy of the debt 109-13

McNamara, Robert 30
manufactures as proportion of exports 19, 22
MAPRALS (Materias Primas de América Latina) 16-23, 110-12
Martin, Preston 107*n*
mass society 101-2*n*
Mena, A.O. 47-8
Mexico 82, 106; growth of debt 7-8, 10, 12-13, 15; imports 70-2, 75, 81; and non-concessional loans 29; pollution in 85-6; renegotiation of debt 108; responsibility for debt 45-8; social imbalance in 57-61, 66
mineral reserves 89-92, 97, 106
mineral resources: depletion of 3-4, 16-25, 42-3, 74, 89-92; prices of 62, 90*n*, 109-10, 112-13; *see also* commodity prices
multinationals 107, 116; banks 9-11, 15, 26, 29-30; and development patterns 2-3, 6, 32; and pollution 86-7

National Wildlife Federation (US) 104
New International Economic Order (NIEO) 94, 98
newly industrialized country (NIC) 3
non-concessional loans 9-11

oil prices 7, 19-21, 29, 106, 108; collapse 27, 41-2
oil reserves 106
OPEC (Oil Producing and Exporting Countries) 42*n*

Peru: growth of debt 10, 12-13, 105; hostility to IMF 37; responsibility for debt 46, 52-3, 74
pesticides 86-7

pollution 2, 84-7, 97-9
Portillo, José López 46
precious metals speculation 39-40
private banks 9-11, 15, 26, 29-30
propaganda and the myth of progress 100-4

raw materials: depletion 3-4, 16-25, 42-3, 74, 89-92; prices 62, 90*n*, 109-10, 112-13; *see also* commodity prices
Reagan, Ronald 40, 42

SDRs (Special Drawing Rights) 34
short-term debt 8, 15-16
social waste 45, 51-83
soil erosion 2, 23-4, 87-9
Special Drawing Rights (SDRs) 34
stand-by credits 35-6
Steinbeck, John: *Grapes of Wrath* 62
structural adjustment loans 38

technological development 101, 103-4, 117-18
toxic wastes 85-7
transnationals *see* multinationals
trickle-down theory 28

United Nations: Economic Commission on Latin America (CEPAL/ECLA) 11-14, 28, 38, 98*n*; Environment Programme 88; World Health Organization (WHO) 85-7
United States: adverse role in Third World 2, 43; dollar fluctuations 39-41, 47; and multinational financial institutions 38; Natural Resources Defense Council 86; water consumption 93
urbanization 2, 84, 88-9

Velsicol Chemical Corporation 87*n*
Venezuela 10; growth of debt 10, 12-13; responsibility for debt 45-6
Volcker, Paul 39-41, 107*n*

water: depletion 92-3; pollution 84-5
World Bank 6, 25, 107; *Development Report 1985* 8-11; role of 32-3, 37-8, 108
World Watch Institute 62

Yom Kippur War 3, 7

zero growth 96-7